Picchu Inca Treasure

Then up the ladder of the earth I climbed
through the barbed jungle's thickets
until I reached you Machu Picchu.

. . .

Mother of stone sperm of condors.
High reef of the human dawn.
Spade buried in primordial sand.

Pablo Neruda

TRANSLATED BY
STEPHEN LIGHT

Cover photograph: Courtesy Giancarlo Ligabue
Photo previous pages: Courtesy Heinz Plenge

FEDERICO KAUFFMANN-DOIG

MACHU PICCHU
INCA TREASURE

Lima, Perú 2006

"Machu Picchu. Inca Treasure" / Federico Kauffmann Doig

First Edition 2006 © Federico Kauffmann Doig.
Editorial Project Nº 11501010500780 / 6000 copies
Edited by © Federico Kauffmann Doig

ISBN Number   9972-9275-2-0
Legal Deposit   2005-9087

Printed by Editora & Comercializadora CARTOLAN E.I.R.L.
Jr. Huiracocha 1733 - 1735, Lima 11 – 4634767

Translation
Stephen Light (Website: www.languageisculture.com)

Sponsor
Puerto Palmeras / Tarapoto Resort

Layout Milton Zevallos
Book Design Federico Kauffmann Doig

Contents

Acknowledgements

The author would like to thank the following people and institutions for their valuable contributions during the writing of this book:

Víctor Angles	Germán Krüger	Hugo Sánchez Santome
Carlos Araníbar	José Landeo	Rose Schnaufer
Percy Ardiles	Adolfo La Rosa	Gustavo Siles
Eduardo Arrarte Fiedler	Vincent Lee	Justo Torres
Rubén Aucahuasi	Giancarlo Ligabue	María del Carmen Unyon Chia
Manuel Bryce Moncloa	Ruperto Márquez	Alfredo Valencia
Daniel Buck	Juan Ossio	Gely Vilca
Eduardo W. Buse	Graciela Chávez de Paz	Kenneth Wright
Atilio Caipani	Heinz Plenge	Walter Wust
Darwin Camacho	Nelly de Romero	Milton Zevallos
Ralph Cané	Roberto Samanez	

BANCO DE CRÉDITO DEL PERÚ / Álvaro Carulla, Luis Nieri, Patricia Usátegui
CÁMARA DE COMERCIO PERUANO-ALEMANA / Georg von Wedemeyer
CONCYTEC / Benjamín Maticorena
COOPERACIÓN ALEMANA AL DESARROLLO (GTZ) / Helmut Eger
EL COMERCIO / Alejandro Miró Quesada Cisneros
GEOGRÁFICA / Heinz Plenge Pardo
GRUPO VIDA / Joël Evrard
ICPNA (Instituto Cultural Peruano-Norteamericano) / Germán Krüger
PROM PERU / Gabriela Trujillo Württele
RUMBOS de Sol & Piedra / Mariela Goyenechea
TARAPOTO HOTEL / Puerto Palmeras / Carlos A. González Henriquez
TREKPERU / Carlos Ruiz
WRIGHT WATER ENGINEERS, INC (Denver, Colorado)

Presentation

Peru has an ancient and rich archaeological legacy crowned by Machu Picchu, the superb monument which the distinguished Peruvian archaeologist Dr. Federico Kauffmann Doig describes and analyses with his customary rigour in this volume.

But although it is undoubtedly the most emblematic monument of Peru's ancient past, Machu Picchu is not the whole story...

In fact, Peru possesses an overwhelming archaeological heritage spread throughout its extensive territory. One fine example is the Northern Amazon Circuit, which offers imposing remains such as Kuelap, a monument to the Chachapoyas culture comprising an immense mountain-top platform no less than six hundred metres long and surrounded by walls up to nineteen metres high in places, as well as natural scenery of such incomparable beauty that the visitor is left with the impression that paradise exists...

Laguna Azul and its neighbour Lake Lindo alone are all the proof one needs that paradise exists... Both of these natural marvels are accessed via Tarapoto on the North Amazon Circuit, and boast many species of tropical birds and a delightful pristine environment.

The natural beauty of the North Amazon Circuit and the splendour of Kuelap can take nothing away from the majesty of Machu Picchu, but anyone who travels this less well-known route will leave convinced that paradise exists in this remote region of Peru.

Carlos González Henríquez
Director General

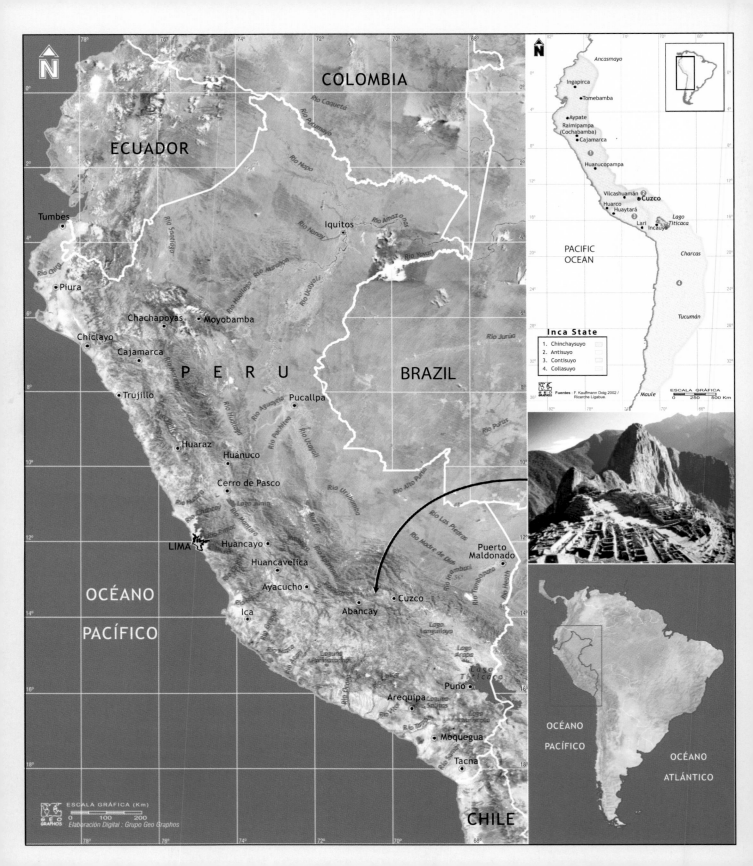

COLOMBIA

ECUADOR

Tumbés

Piura

Chiclayo

Cajamarca

Trujillo

Chachapoyas   Moyobamba

P E R U

Huaraz

Huánuco

Cerro de Pasco

Lago Junin

LIMA   Huancayo

Huancavelica

Ayacucho

Ica

Abancay   Cuzco

OCÉANO

PACÍFICO

Arequipa

Puno

Moquegua

Tacna

CHILE

BRAZIL

Iquitos

Pucallpa

Puerto
Maldonado

Lago
Langunlayo

Lago
Arapa

Lago
Titicaca

Río Caquetá

Río Putumayo

Río Napo

Río Amazonas

Río Nanay

Río Yavarí

Río Juruá

Río Purús

Río Las Piedras

Río Madre de Dios

Río Alto Purús

Río Heath

Río Santiago

Río Chira

Río Marañon

Río Huallaga

Río Ucayali

Río Aguaytia

Río Pachitea

Río Urubamba

Río Mantaro

Río Ene

Río Tambopata

Río Grande

Río Acarí

Río Ocoña

Río Tambo

Laguna
Parinacochas

Laguna
Salinas

ESCALA GRÁFICA (Km)
0   100   200
Elaboración Digital : Grupo Geo Graphos

Ancasmayo

Ingapirca

Tomebamba

Aypate
Raimipampa
(Cochabamba)   Cajamarca

Huanucopampa

Vilcashuamán   Cuzco
Huarco   Huaytará
Lari
Incauyo   Lago
Titicaca

PACIFIC
OCEAN

Charcas

Tucumán

Maule

Inca State
1. Chinchaysuyo
2. Antisuyo
3. Contisuyo
4. Collasuyo

ESCALA GRÁFICA
0   250   500 Km

Fuentes : F. Kauffmann Doig 2002 /
Ricerche Ligabue.

OCÉANO
PACÍFICO

OCÉANO
ATLÁNTICO

Machu Picchu lies at the heart of a landscape of imposing peaks covered with luxuriant vegetation. It was built sometime in the last third of the 15th century by the Incas, whose culture was the final phase of six thousand years of Peruvian civilization. In common with other similar monuments of the period, it was built in relative proximity to Cuzco, in the land of Vilcabamba, a region of rugged slopes and cloud forest typical of the Amazonian Andes.

Although the details of its past may never be clarified, we can assume that its main functions were those of an administrative centre for the production of the crops grown on its steep terraces and, at the same time, a religious centre dedicated to the gods upon whom its inhabitants believed their existence depended: the God of Water and Mother Earth, or Pachamama.(*)

Together with other agrarian centres in the Vilcabamba region, Machu Picchu must have been conceived within the context of a huge state project, the object of which was the extension of agricultural activity into the Amazonian Andes beyond Cuzco. This hypothesis is based on the fact that in Peru land suitable for agriculture is scarce, both in the highlands and coastal Andes. Since the dawn of Andean civilization, soils have proved inadequate in the face of growing population density, in common with all ancient societies that chose to live from agriculture. On the other hand, this ecological imbalance inspired the development of diverse strategies aimed at solving the problem of food production, including the expansion of agrarian frontiers.

(*) This proposal rests on careful research, based on related information and ethnographic testimonies, as well as archaeological-iconographic observation and the study of ethno-historical sources (Kauffmann-Doig 1986a; 1991b; 1996a; 2001a; 2001c; 2003a and 2003b)

To the problem of extremely limited land for cultivation, another factor has always affected food production in Peru and brought hunger to its people: the El Niño phenomenon, which regularly unleashes periods of drought and flooding, as well as other meteorological calamities.

It was believed that such catastrophes could only be prevented through magical-religious practices; the worship of the supernatural entity that controls atmospheric phenomena. This was the God of Water, the most important deity in the Andean pantheon, present in the Apus, or high mountains, who was called upon to fertilize Mother Earth by drenching her with his rains. These divine beings are still venerated throughout large areas of the Peruvian highlands. In short, as well as being an administrative centre for food production, Machu Picchu was built as a religious site for the practice of rituals aimed at propitiating the gods upon whom the harvest depended. This hypothesis will be discussed at length in a separate chapter, as will a number of other theories that attempt to explain the enigma of Machu Picchu's role in ancient Peru.

Federico Kauffmann-Doig

Machu Picchu:
Treasure of Inca Architecture

Machu Picchu (Matshu Piktshu), the jewel of Inca architecture, is one of the wonders of the world. Because it expresses the ability of man to build in harmony with the imposing scenery that surrounds it, UNESCO has declared the ruins a World Heritage Site in both its cultural and natural categories.

Machu Picchu, together with other neighbouring sites built in a similar style, is located in the Machu Picchu Historical Sanctuary, created in 1981 and covering an area of 35,592 hectares (INRENA 1999;

Muelle, Bonavia and Chávez Ballón 1972). These ruins lie in a superb landscape of steep slopes covered in luxuriant jungle vegetation and crowned by great snow-covered peaks. Altitudes within the Sanctuary range from 2000 to 6000 metres above sea level, making it home to an extraordinary biodiversity.

Machu Picchu stands on the heights above the left bank of the Urubamba river, at 2400 metres above sea level. The buildings and agricultural terraces occupy a narrow and uneven saddle,

between the peaks of Huayna Picchu (Waina Piktshu) and Machu Picchu. Both rest on a perpendicular geological formation which has created precipices that fall away to the raging waters of the Urubamba river 400 metres below, where the river forms a crescent-shaped meander, hugging the hills of Huayna Picchu and Machu Picchu.

The monument is reached from Cuzco by train. The Puente Ruinas station is 112.5 kilometres from the ancient imperial capital. From the station, a zigzag road climbs to the ruins. Machu Picchu can also be accessed via the ancient Inca Trail, which begins at Qoriwayrachina (Qoriwairatshina) at Km.88 of the railway line, or at Piscacucho (Piskakutsho) at Km.82. On foot, the trail takes between three and four days to complete. The trek along this and other Inca Trails leading to Machu Picchu not only permits one to enjoy the imposing scenery, but also to admire magnificent archaeological sites such as Phuyupatamarka (Phuiupatamarka) and Wiñay Wayna (Winiai Waina).

Machu Picchu is usually translated as "Old Peak" (*machu* = old, *picchu* = peak or hill). Given that this name refers to its geography, it is unlikely to have been the original name of the city. Also, the word *picchu*

does not appear in the first Quechua dictionaries, such as that of Diego González Holguín (1608) or the more recent edition by Ernst W. Middendorf (1890-1892, v.2), which may mean that the word is a corruption of the Spanish *pico*, meaning the peak or summit of a hill. González Holguín translates "summit" as *orcop uman* (head of hill), as does Middendorf, who spells it *orkoj uman*. The word *Picho* or *Piccho*, in reference to Machu Picchu, first appears in some recently discovered 16th century documents (Glave and Remy 1983, Rowe 1990, Varón 1993), but it does not appear in the aforementioned dictionaries under "summit" or "peak". José Uriel García (1961b) and José G. Cosio (1912) challenge the definition "peak" for *picchu* and, taking for granted that

Machu Picchu was the original name of the city, suggest that it may be a neuter noun "derived from the verb *picchay*" (the act of chewing coca).

Machu Picchu has become the proud emblem of Peru's national identity (Flores Ochoa 2004; Karp de Toledo 2004b). Without a doubt, it will continue to provoke the admiration of the world for as long as it is properly conserved. The site must be protected from tectonic movement affecting the sub-soils on which the walls rest (Bouchard et al. 1992; Carlotto and Cárdenas 2001; Kalafatovich 1963; Kauffmann-Doig 2001b) and new strategies need to be developed to cushion the negative effects of mass tourism, the growth of which threatens to overwhelm the city (INRENA 1999).

▶

The wives of the peasants Melquiades Richarte and Anacleto Álvarez, who when Bingham reached Machu Picchu were growing crops on some of the terraces
Photo Hiram Bingham (1912)

▶

Hiram Bingham (1875 – 1956)

Machu Picchu in July 1912, at the start of the expedition led by Bingham
Photo Hiram Bingham (1912) / Hugh Thomson 2001

Chapter 2
Bingham's Discovery
and its Antecedents

His search for the legendary city of Vilcabamba (Wilkapanpa), the last stronghold of the Inca kings who took refuge in the inhospitable Vilcabamba region between 1536 and 1572, led Hiram Bingham (1875-1956), an historian and Yale professor, to reveal the existence of Machu Picchu to the entire world.

In 1911, Bingham arrived in Cuzco in search of the lost city of the Incas. His plan was to go deep into the region beyond the headwaters of the Vilcabamba, which flows into the Urubamba at Chaullay. Before beginning his journey, he received information in Cuzco regarding Machu Picchu. Because these reports indicated that the ruins were on the route he would have to follow to reach Vilcabamba, Bingham stopped at Mandorbamba, from where he reached the ruins. He remained for just one day, and decided that these could not be the ruins of the citadel he was searching for, for their location did not coincide with the descriptions in the historical sources he had consulted, such as the chronicles of Friar Antonio de la Calancha (1638).

At Mandorbamba, Bingham interviewed the peasant Melchor Arteaga, who confirmed the magnitude of the ruins of Machu Picchu, of which Albert Giesecke had spoken to him in Cuzco. Astonished by Arteaga's account, Bingham asked him to guide him in return for a financial reward. Accompanied by Arteaga and Sergeant Carrasco, the policeman assigned to him, the American climbed the steep, forested slopes sep-

The Urubamba river and Putucusi mountain from Machu Picchu
Photo: Quintin Huamani

arating Mandorbamba from the ruins. The discovery of Machu Picchu occurred on June 24th, 1911. Until then, this treasure of Inca architecture had remained hidden from the world, apart from the occasional treasure hunter and the peasants who lived nearby, as Bingham himself pointed out in his writings. Bingham tells how, on arriving at the ruins, he was met by members of the two peasant families who lived there. They had established themselves just a few years previously, and were growing their crops on some of the site's ancient terraces, not far from their huts. It was a boy named Pablito Álvarez who led Bingham to where the imposing walls of Machu Picchu rose from the dense tropical vegetation that half covered them. Astonished, Bingham scribbled the following phrase in his journal: "Would anyone believe what I have found…?".

According to Bingham himself, (1913, 1949 p.264), thirty years had passed since, guided by rumours, the illustrious traveller Charles Wiener (1851-1913) had attempted to reach Machu Picchu, in his role as an explorer with the official backing of both Peru and Bolivia, from 1876 to 1877. In the map of the "Vallée de Santa Ana", which he included in his book *Perou et Bolivie*, he places the names *Matchopicchu* and *Huaynapicchu* with astonishing precision, thanks to the information supplied to him by those who lived nearby (Wiener 1880). Daniel Buck has referred to an even older cartographical reference unknown to Bingham. He refers to the names Machu Picchu and Huaina Picchu that appear in the "Map of the Valleys of Paucartambo, Lares, Ocobamba and the Vilcanota Canyon", produced by Herman Göhring (Göhring 1877) and discussed by Buck (1993 p.29) in a study examining the debate as to who reached Machu Picchu first. Ten years after its publication, the map was reedited by Mariana Mould de Pease (2003) and a detail published in order to highlight the references to Machu Picchu and Huayna Picchu.

Bingham describes how in Cuzco he was informed of a trip to Machu Picchu made in 1902 by Agustín Lizárraga in the company of two peasant friends. He adds that in Cuzco Lizárraga "sold one or two ceramics he claimed came from Machu Picchu" (Bingham 1949, p.261). Nevertheless, writing of those who preceded him, Yazmín López believes that Bingham tried to silence Lizárraga. What is certain, however, is that Bingham not only mentions Lizárraga repeatedly in his writings, but also describes the inscription left by the latter carved "on a wall of one of the most beautiful buildings", graffiti which he quite rightly had removed.

In Cuzco it is said that before Lizárraga, in around 1894, Luis Béjar Ugarte reached Machu Picchu (Buck 1993). It should be pointed out, however, that those who arrived before Bingham did so with no scientific purpose in mind. The two families living at the ruins were there to feed themselves by using some sectors of the old terracing. And the occasional visitors

Pablito Álvarez, the boy from one of the two families that Bingham found in 1911 when he reached Machu Picchu. It was Pablito who led Bingham to the ruins. He was eleven years old at the time: "Richarte and Álvarez sent a child to guide me…" (Bingham)
Photo: Hiram Bingham

▶ The Shrine of Ñustaispana discovered by Bingham. It is located in the Vitcos area, near Huancacalle in the Vilcabamba valley
Photo: Federico Kauffmann Doig

▶ Remains of the Inca's Residence, located in the Vitcos area and explored for the first time by Bingham. Shown in a photo taken around 1980, before restoration work
Photo: Courtesy Víctor Angles

to the site before Bingham, whom many describe as the "real discoverers of Machu Picchu", were motivated by the possibility of hidden treasure. José Gabriel Cosio (1912) proclaimed: "Machupiccho has been visited by many, but it owes its celebrity to Dr. Bingham".

Indisputably, it was Albert Giesecke (1885-1968), the campaigner for university education and culture in Cuzco, who told Bingham how to reach Machu Picchu, on the route chosen by the latter in his search for the neo-Inca bastion of Vilcabamba. Giesecke (1961, p.17) writes that Bingham "was often at my house before leaving Cuzco". Giesecke himself, just a year before Bingham's arrival, had journeyed to Machu Picchu. Accompanied by Braulio Polo y La Borda, one of the owners of the Echarati hacienda, he travelled

"Mister Happiness", as Bingham and his companions called him, thanks to his permanent smile. He was one of the workers who, in 1912, helped to clear the vegetation that covered the ruins of Machu Picchu
Photo: Hiram Bingham

through the Urubamba valley as far as Mandorbamba, at the foot of Machu Picchu hill. There they met Melchor Arteaga – the key figure Bingham would later seek out – who was to lead them to the ruins. Intense rains, however, thwarted Giesecke's expedition.

The fact that Bingham himself describes such antecedents casts in a most favourable light the academic seriousness with which he conducted his explorations. For that reason, although he was not the first to reach the site, there can be no denying the fact that he was the real scientific discoverer of Machu Picchu and the pioneer in research related to the ruins. It was Bingham who, conscious of the importance of its architecture, revealed to the world this exceptional legacy of Peru's ancient inhabitants. It was in vain that Carl Haenel attempted to discredit Bingham by claiming in 1916 that Machu Picchu had been discovered years earlier by the explorer Georg von Hassel (Buck 1993). Nor was the American explorer's prestige damaged by fallacious reports in the European press claiming that the true discoverer of Machu Picchu was the English missionary Thomas Ernest Payne

(Buck 1993). Mariana Mould de Pease (2003) leads the current movement to discredit Bingham as the scientific discoverer, describing him as merely the "scientific informant".

After the initial criticisms he made in 1915 in the newspaper El Sol de Cuzco (Camacho 2004), pp.43-46), the distinguished academic Luis E. Valcárcel wrote (Valcárcel 1964, p68), in an apparent effort to do justice to Bingham: "As happens with all discoveries, there were precursors. In this case, those precursors were individuals incapable of appreciating the value of the monument before their eyes. It would be narrow minded not to acknowledge the first person to realise the great value of what he had discovered. Bingham knew what he was looking for and his discovery was not mere chance. He was a Professor of American History at Yale who had taken a deep interest in the study of the Inca empire, and in particular research into the last stronghold of the Incas, the region ruled by the so-called "Incas of Vilcabamba". Not satisfied with the references in the chronicles, he delved into the documentary sources in the archives and built the necessary bibliography".

▶
Map showing the routes followed by the Bingham expeditions
Map by Hugh Thomson 2001

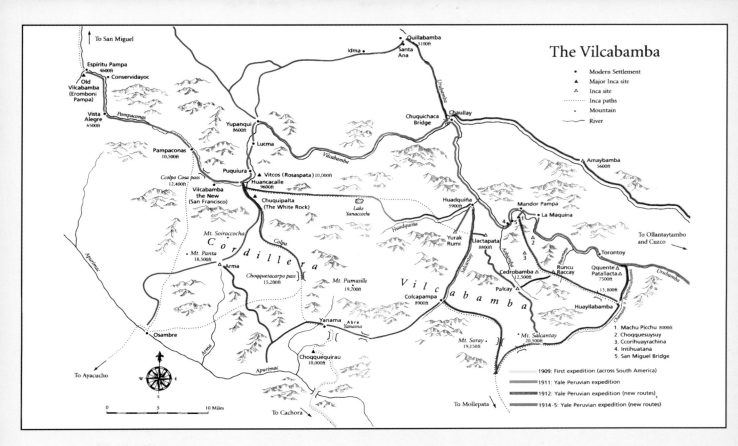

The Vilcabamba

- • Modern Settlement
- ▲ Major Inca site
- △ Inca site
- ⋯⋯ Inca paths
- • Mountain
- — River

1. Machu Picchu 8000ft
2. Choqquesuysuy
3. Ccorihuayrachina
4. Intihuatana
5. San Miguel Bridge

1909: First expedition (across South America)
1911: Yale Peruvian expedition
1912: Yale Peruvian expedition (new routes)
1914-5: Yale Peruvian expedition (new routes)

Chapter 3
Bingham's Expeditions

Bingham's first contact with Machu Picchu in 1911 was brief, for his main objective was to identify the lost city of Vilcabamba the Old which, according to his calculations, could not be located at the site occupied by Machu Picchu He returned a year later, in 1912, at the head of a scientific expedition sponsored by Yale University and the National Geographic Society and boasting several distinguished scientists. He returned to Peru again in 1914-15 to explore the area around the ruins,

including the Inca roads leading to the site, travelling almost the entire route now known as the Inca Trail from Corihuairachina to Machu Picchu. Bingham (1915) mentions that on that occasion his guide was Ricardo Charaja, whom he warmly praises. Along the route he explored several ruins situated in the vicinity of the Inca road, such as Patallacta (Pataiaqta), Runturacay (Runturaqai-i) and Sayakmarka (Saiaqmarka), which, in accordance with information supplied by Charaja, he

named Cedrobamba. He also charged Clarence Maynard with inspecting the archaeological remains located on the left bank of the Urubamba river, including Chachabamba (Tshatshpanpa) and Choquesuisuy (Tschoqesuisui). Years later, in 1940-41, Paul Fejos made a careful study of those sites (Fejos 1944).
Bingham visited Peru in 1909, before his first visit to Machu Picchu. Passing through Cuzco, he headed for Abancay, where the governor of the Apurímac region encouraged him to seek

▲

"It is likely that the stone bench where my Indian helper rests was made for the mummies of the ancient Incas…" (Bingham)
Photo: Hiram Bingham

▲

Bingham guessed that these two sculptured receptacles were mortars "to grind freeze-dried potatoes or corn". They were probably water mirrors with a magical significance
Photo: Hiram Bingham

▶

According to Bingham, these niches in the Prison Group, "held the mummies of important dignitaries". Another theory, although unproven, is that the holes in some of the ashlars held the wrists of prisoners condemned to torture
Photo: Hiram Bingham 1912

Drawing by George F. Eaton of some of the tombs excavated in 1912, beneath the subsoil of a terrace and roofed by an enormous rock
Drawing: G.F. Eaton (1912)

▼ Plan of the aforementioned terrace with the location of the skeletons recovered
G.F. Eaton (1912)

▼ Cranium excavated at Machu Picchu during the Bingham expeditions and published by Richard L. Burger. Note the pronounced deformation of the skull
Photo: John Verano

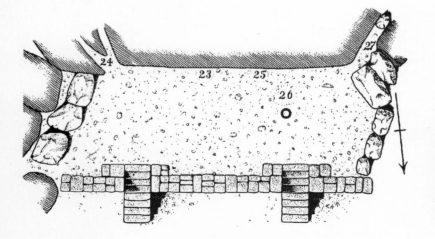

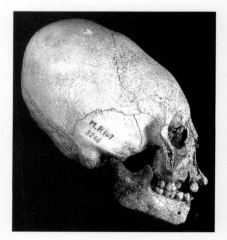

the treasures presumed to lie hidden at Choquequirao (Tshok-kekirao), an important archaeological site situated high above the right bank of the Apurímac river. Bingham was surprised to discover that the local governor failed to understand that his was not a treasure-seeking mission. Nevertheless, Bingham took the opportunity to map the site of Choquequirao for the first time (Bingham 1910).

Based on his expeditions of 1909, 1911, 1912 and 1914-15, Bingham published several studies of Machu Picchu (Bingham 1912a, 1912b, 1913, 1915a, 1915b). In 1930 he produced his major work; *Machu Picchu: A Citadel of the Incas*. Years later, he would publish extracts from this book in popular editions that sold well and would make Machu Picchu world famous (Bingham 1948, 1953).

Although the excavations made by Bingham at Machu Picchu almost a century ago can be criticised today for their methodology – just as today's work is likely to be criticised by future generations of archaeologists – its multi-disciplinary nature should be underlined, together with the fact that several experts were members of the team. In this sense Bingham's work remains unequalled, for subsequent studies have been the result of individual researchers and aimed principally at conservation of the site. The scientists who accompanied Bingham on his 1912 and 1914-15 expeditions were: K.C. Heald, engineer; George Eaton, osteologist; Herbert E. Gregory, geologist; Ellwood Charles Erdis, archaeologist; Albert H. Bumstead, geographer; Isahia Bowman, the celebrated geographer and author of *The Southern Andes*; H.W. Foot and O.F. Cook, botanists; Phillip Ainsworth Means, historian; H.L. Tucker, engineer/archaeologist; Kay Hendrickson, topographer; Luther Nelson and W.G. Irving, surgeons; Robert Stephenson, Paul Osgood Hardy, Joseph Little Prescott and P. Lanius, auxiliary staff; Paul Bestor and P.B. Lanins, secretaries. The expedition was accompanied by the Cuzco engineer Carlos A. Duque. In addition: David Ford, Edmund Heller, E.L. Anderson, Clarence F. Maynard, J.J. Haasbrouk, G. Bruce Gilbert and G.H. Morkill joined the last phase of the expedition. Dominique R. Lacerte (2000) has produced biographies of those who accompanied the 1911 and 1912 expeditions.

Mariana Mould Pease (2003) emphasises the fact that Bingham, apart from that which he removed in 1914-15, never returned to Peru the material found at Machu Picchu. She describes him as a man of dubious ethics, and refers to a few passages taken from intimate family conversations and revealed by one of his sons, Alfred Bingham (1987, 1989). Other authors who have followed a similar vein of character assassination include: Luis Barreda Murillo (2001), Darwin Camacho Paredes (2004), Yazmín López (2004), Jorge Riveros Cayo (2004), and others.

▶

Start of the research work of 1912 at Machu Picchu. To the right Lieutenant Sotomayor, with a baton in his hand, directs the work.
Photo: Hiram Bingham

Chapter 4

Machu Picchu:
The Material Excavated by the Bingham Expeditions

Although they lacked the professional methods current today, their excavations brought Bingham and his scientists some 555 pieces of pottery, almost 220 bronze, copper, tin and silver artifacts and thousands of fragments of human and animal bones (Valcárcel 1964). Most of the objects were found during the 1912 expedition in tombs set into natural caves. The most outstanding pieces, kept at the Peabody Museum of Natural History at Yale University, were first published by Bing-

ham (1915a, 1930), and more recently by Lucy C. Salazar and Richard L. Burger (2004), in a catalogue that includes material not found at Machu Picchu but acquired by Bingham, as well as other archaeological objects included in the exhibition they organised.

Among the pieces exhumed by Bingham there figure examples of the finest pottery (Bingham 1915b). The specimens of metal, especially bronze, show the high degree of skill achieved by Inca metalworkers (Gordon 1986;

Matthewson 1915 Rutledge and Gordon 1987). They include bracelets, ear adornments, knives, axes and *tupus*, brooches for fastening small *llicllas*, or shawls. Other objects were also found, including a collection of 156 small ceramic and stone discoid plates, "a batch of 42 oblong stones of green schist no more than three centimetres long and two centimetres wide and 19 triangular counters (…), mortars and decorated stone boxes, hammers and carved bones". The list of findings (Valcárcel

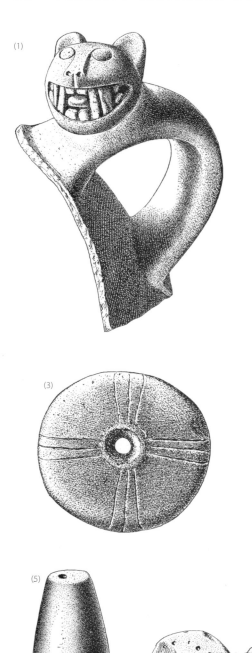

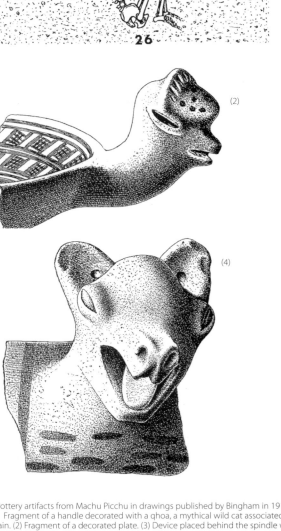

Pottery artifacts from Machu Picchu in drawings published by Bingham in 1915: (1) Fragment of a handle decorated with a qhoa, a mythical wild cat associated with rain. (2) Fragment of a decorated plate. (3) Device placed behind the spindle which helps to twist the thread during spinning. (4) Fragment of a receptacle, apparently decorated with the head of a llama. (5) Whistle or small flute. (6) Ear decoration worn on the lower part of the ear

Drawings published by Bingham for the first time in 1915

Receptacle found in Tomb 26 excavated by George F. Eaton, together with other pieces of pottery and the skeleton of a dog. The body had been buried with its legs bent and wrapped in textiles
Photo: Yale University, New Haven

A 0.64 metre tall receptacle, or "aríbalo". The
motifs represent the water emblem in the form of
the crest of a wave, together with stylised birds.
These jars were carried on the shoulder, as seen
in the photograph of a Chimu-Inca ceramic
Drawings published by Bingham in 1915
Photo: Staatliche Museen zu Berlin-Preussischer
Kulturbesitz / Museum für Volkerkunde
Courtesy Banco de Crédito del Perú

Five ceramics excavated intact in
1912 by the Yale University expedition
led by Bingham
Drawings published by Bingham in 1915

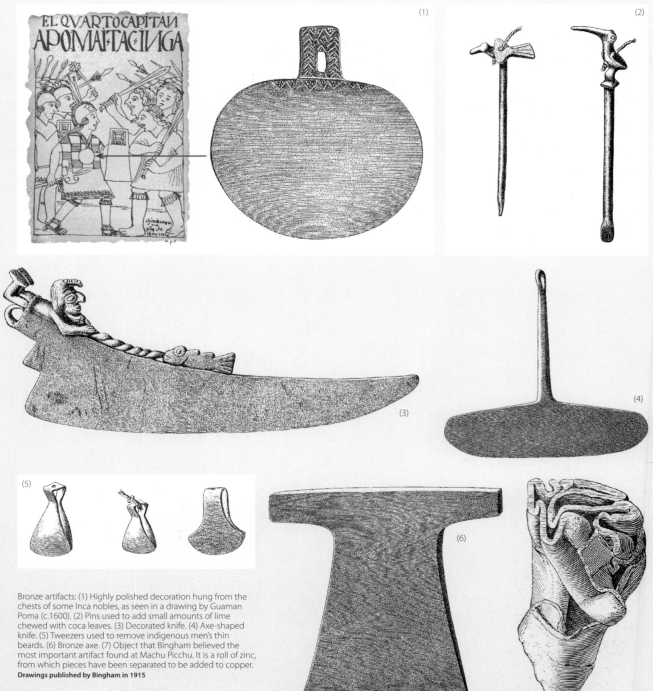

Bronze artifacts: (1) Highly polished decoration hung from the chests of some Inca nobles, as seen in a drawing by Guaman Poma (c.1600). (2) Pins used to add small amounts of lime chewed with coca leaves. (3) Decorated knife. (4) Axe-shaped knife. (5) Tweezers used to remove indigenous men's thin beards. (6) Bronze axe. (7) Object that Bingham believed the most important artifact found at Machu Picchu. It is a roll of zinc, from which pieces have been separated to be added to copper.
Drawings published by Bingham in 1915

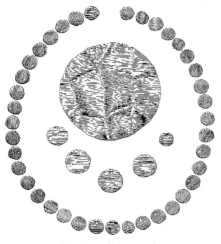

Discoid metal plates used
in the making of necklaces

1964, pp. 81-82) from the Machu Picchu collection at the Peabody Museum also includes three stone sculptures, but they were not found at the site. In fact, the majority of the pieces acquired by Bingham were not found at Machu Picchu (Salazar and Burger 2004).

A very large number of bone fragments – both animal and human – were found at Machu Picchu. The bones were exhumed by Elwood Erdis and George F. Eaton. After being studied by Eaton (1916) and Charles W. Goff (1966), the bones at the Peabody were analysed by George R. Miller (2003) and John W. Verano (2003).

The material removed by Bingham during his 1914-15 excavations was returned to Peru in several boxes, some of which were very large. There were a total of 74 boxes (Mould 2003). Some of the boxes are now deposited at the National Museum of Archaeology, Anthropology and History of Peru. Although

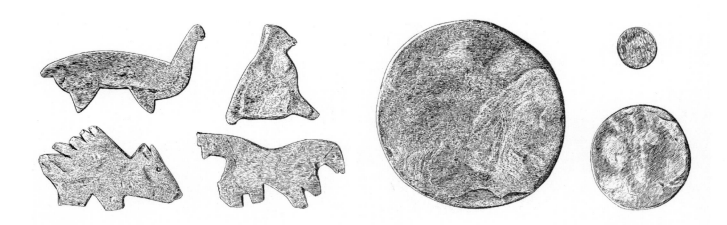

(1)

(2)

(3)

Carved stone objects: (1) Coffer carved from a single block, decorated with symbolic figures which are repeated and appear to represent emblems associated with water. Length 0.42 m. (2) Small animal figures. (3) Discoid representations perhaps intended to mimic Spanish coins, to which a magical value may have been attached
Drawings published by Bingham 1915

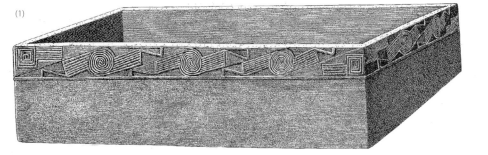

Carved bone, probably a brooch for a lliclla (liklia) or woman's shawl. It portrays two converging birds and circles symbolising rain drops

the research department ordered that the boxes be opened in 1980 for inventory and analysis, the order was not carried out, and they remained sealed until 1984, when they were opened and the material transferred to cardboard boxes. Finally, in 2002, the archaeologist Fanny Montesinos produced an inventory (Mould 2003, pp.171-173). Previously, in 2001 and 2002, Ken Ichi Shinoda was given access to a part of the dental remains for DNA analysis, just as Sara Gheler had been under Professor Robert Benfer in 1976-77, as part of her university thesis (Personal information / Dr. Hilda Vidal 2003).

The results are still unknown, and it is time that all the material returned to Peru by Bingham be located and the relevant studies undertaken. The batch housed at the Peabody Museum, already analysed by the anthropologist George F. Eaton in 1916, and under the care of Richard L. Burger since 1981 (Burger and Salazar 2003 p. XIV), should also be subjected to further tests, as many specialists such as Verano and Miller have stated in their published work.

The material handed over to the Peabody was never part of Bingham's private collection. It was handed over in its entirety to the Peabody Museum of Yale University. Mariana Mould de Pease (2003) insists that under the terms of the contract they should have been returned and were not. Of course, the material ought to be repatriated eventually, and Peru's National Institute of Culture (INC) should assume responsibility for the preservation and custodianship of the remains and guarantee that there be no repeat of the scandalous robberies perpetrated in the nation's museums with impunity, such as the incident in 1979, when 4,400 metal artifacts were stolen. The INC should also turn its attention to the corruption within its own walls, which led to the depredation of the invaluable cultural heritage discovered at the Lake of the Mummies, or Lake of the Condors, when documents were falsified with the involvement of individuals from the very highest echelons of the National Institute of Culture (INC).

▶

Gold bracelet, the only gold object found to date at Machu Picchu. It was discovered in 1995 during excavations in one of the plazas.
Photo: Courtesy Wright Water Engineers, Denver Colorado / USA

Chapter 5
Research
and Restoration Work after Bingham

Since the Bingham expeditions of 1911, 1912 and 1914-15, the main objectives of scholars have been centred around repair and conservation to satisfy the expectations of the growing tourist economy. Luis A. Pardo (1961a) has written on the work of this kind carried out between 1939 and 1966, as have Alfredo Valencia and Arminda Gibaja (1992), whose study examines the issue since Bingham's time.

Many individuals have been involved in restoration, and not always successfully

(Araoz 2001; Wurster 2001). The restoration work of Marino Sánchez Macedo (1990), as well as that of other archaeologists, may be considered satisfactory, together with that of Wilbert San Román Luna from 1985 to 1987 (San Román 2001).

The research carried out after Bingham has been documented by Alfredo Valencia and Arminda Gibaja (1992), and Fernando Astete Victoria (2001) has dealt with the work done between 1994 and 2000. In general terms, research has

been limited when compared to restoration work. Alfredo Valencia (1977) excavated at the Sacred Rock sector (here known as the "Replica of the Apus") and Julinho Zapata Rodríguez (1983) worked, for his thesis, on the so-called Military Sector. Astronomical observations have also been made (White and Dearborn 1980) and some samples from the site have been subjected to radiocarbon dating (Berger et al. 1988). In the field of research, the studies and valuable conclusions reached by

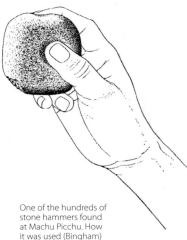

One of the hundreds of stone hammers found at Machu Picchu. How it was used (Bingham)
Drawings Hiram Bingham

the Wright Water Engineers company between 1995 and 1999 deserve special mention (Valencia 2004). Research was centred on the water supply at Machu Picchu and was carried out jointly by American specialists and the Peruvian Alfredo Valencia Zegarra. The Wright Water Engineers researchers have published a copious bibliography, to which we will refer subsequently, and which highlights the contribution of Kenneth R. Wright. For his part, Manuel Chavez Ballón, aside from his conservation work (1971), has shown an interest in the analysis of pottery from Machu Picchu (Chávez 1955, 1961).

The cultural material recovered after Bingham can be regarded as poor in the extreme, both in quality and quantity, when compared to the splendid architecture of Machu Picchu. Such were the findings of Fernando Astete Victoria (2001) during his excavations between 1994 and 2000, when he explored the small natural caves used as tombs and exhumed bone fragments in a "terrible state of preservation".

It is interesting to note that the excavations of Astete and the anthropologist Elva Torres seem to "show that the identifiable individuals, in the majority, were male". This valuable conclusion destroys the hypothesis that Machu Picchu was the resting place of predominantly female remains, as proposed by George F. Eaton (1916), which gave rise to several outlandish theories regarding the population of the city (G.F. Eaton 1990). Astete and Torres have made inroads into research regarding agricultural technology. Referring to purely cultural material, Astete states that he recovered 500 stone percussion instruments and hammers, which can be added to those already found by Bingham. He also discovered a half-smelted metal star-shaped club and, like Bingham, a number of ceramic offerings that had been deliberately broken. A singular discovery was that of a 16 carat gold bracelet, found in 1995 in the square "adjacent to the Condor complex".

In the field of interpretation, special mention must be made of the conclusions reached by Johan Reinhard (1991). His work focuses on magical-religious practices that survive to the present day, as well as ethno-historic data, astronomical observations and the majestic scenery surrounding the site. He concludes that in order to understand Machu Picchu's purpose it is necessary to take into account its connection to sacred topography. We will have cause to discuss further Reinhard's hypothesis, together with other theories regarding Machu Picchu's function.

Carmen Bernand / Serge Hochain

Chapter 6
Antiquity
of Machu Picchu

▶
Face of an Inca or neo-Inca on a quero (qero) or ceremonial vase, polychrome, of Inca manufacture after the Spanish conquest (16th century?)
Photo: Pörtner / Davis

The architectural characteristics of Machu Picchu are similar to those found in other Cuzco monuments, which suggests it dates from the same Inca period. Similarly, the archaeological remains excavated belong, in style, to the same period: the so-called Historic Inca, or Expansionist, phase of the second half of the 15th century. If the site dates from this period, we can conclude that it was built during the government of Pachacutec (1438-71). Such conclusions were first proposed by Luis E. Valcárcel

(1964) and have been to some extent confirmed by early writings (Glave and Remy 1983; Rowe 1990). Building work may have continued during the reign of Tupac Inca Yupanqui (1471-93), Pachacutec's successor.

Of course, not all the buildings at the site were constructed at the same time. Wilfredo Yépez Valdéz (2001) believes that some of them were never completed. Nor is it certain that the greater or lesser antiquity of the constructions obeys a gradual linear development

and perfecting of architectural technique. The differences in style within the site are explained by the function of each building, as well as other factors (Kauffmann-Doig 1965).

The hypothesis of José Gabriel Cosio that Machu Picchu was a product of "a Quechua civilization that predates the dynasty of the Children of the Sun..." and that the site was unknown during Inca times can only be classed as implausible. (Cosio 1912/Reed: Chevarría 1992).

Chapter 7

Machu Picchu
Before and After the Inca Empire

When the Incas from the highlands began to occupy the Vilcabamba region, they would have found the high areas such as that occupied by Machu Picchu sparsely populated, otherwise the remains of pre-Inca inhabitants would have been found at Machu Picchu. The region was certainly inhabited since time immemorial by small farm worker communities, as Peter Frost (2004) confirmed with his recent discovery of pre-Inca and Inca pottery around the Inca settlement of Qoriwayrachina, on the slopes of Cerro Victoria, 35 kilometres from Machu Picchu. Some of the findings identified by Frost correspond to a style characterised by anthropomorphic figures with the type of eyes known as "coffee bean". This detail recalls the style of Marcavalle pottery from Cuzco, a formative site discovered by Manuel Chávez Ballón in 1954 (Valencia and Gibaja 1991). According to Karen Mohr-Chávez (1980), who continued the study, Marcavalle dates from the first millennium before Christ, which would confirm that human occupation of the Vilcabamba region not only dates from ancient times, but that the first inhabitants came from the eastern Andes, and not from the Amazon lowlands.

Carbon dating of charcoal recovered from Machu Picchu to 2000 years (Berger, Chofhi, Valencia, Yépez and Fernán-dez 1988), confirms the early occupation of some sectors of the region. The great age of the carbon-dated remains caused confusion in some academic circles, where it was mistakenly supposed that they belonged to the Machu Picchu we know today and which dates from the 15th century.

According to Luis E. Valcárcel (1964), a people related to the Incas of Cuzco, from the *Tampu* ethnic group, occupied the area around Ollantaytambo (Oliantaitanpu). He discounted the possibility of their having come from the highlands rather than Amazonia and states that the *Tampus* did not occupy the heights of their territory, which would rule them out as the builders of Machu Picchu. However, in an initial study (Valcárcel 1961), he postulated that "Machu Picchu belongs to the Inca culture, possessing certain characteristics of the local *Tampu* style", which unfortunately he did not go on to define.

The colonising of the Vilcabamba region by the Incas nourished in the *mitmacs* and the administrators and specialists from Cuzco the art of agricultural engineering. According to a 16th century document brought to light by María Rostworowski (1963, p.237), Tupac Yupanqui was accompanied by Chachapoyans, brought in to help populate the region.

Upon invading the zone, the Incas did not encounter forest dwellers, for Machu Picchu lies at 2,400 metres above sea level and has a very different climate to that favoured by the inhabitants of the lowland forests, known to the Incas as *Chunchos*, who prefer to live no more than 1,000 metres above sea level. There may have been isolated groups of Amazonians in highland areas, at Vitcos for example, where Manco Inca and his successors recruited the archers referred to by the chroniclers (Murúa c.1600; Rodríguez de Figueroa 1565). Scenes on native ceremonial cups, known as *queros*, and made after the arrival of the Spanish, depict battles between Inca troops and Amazonian warriors, and probably represent neo-Inca incursions into the marginal areas between the Andes and the Amazon basin to occupy territory or recruit combatants.

It is to be supposed that Machu Picchu continued to be occupied by successive peasant families through the centuries who would have used the agricultural terracing in an informal manner and with the consent of local landowners. Equally, it is to be assumed that periods of occupation were interspersed with periods of abandonment, as evidenced by the family Bingham found at the site in 1911, who had only been there for a few years.

Reconstruction of how the entrance to the Sacred Sector at Machu Picchu was closed from behind (according to Bingham). This pattern is repeated at Machu Picchu and other Inca archaeological sites

Chapter 8
Machu Picchu:
Architectural Characteristics

Several studies have been made of Inca architecture (Agurto Calvo 1987; Bonavia 1997, 1999; Bengtsson 1998; Bouchard 1991; Harth-terré, 1965; Gallegos 2000, pp.126-179; Kendall 1978, 1988; Protzen 1983, 1985, 1986; Velarde 1946, pp.36-60). Graciano Gasparini and Louise Margolies (1977, 1980) are the authors of a thick and very important study of the principal monuments built during the Inca period.

An overall view of the constructions at Machu Picchu reveals a generally rect-angular shape to most buildings, which are of one storey and form compounds of different sizes. In one case, a *callanca* (kalianka), a large, complex construction designed to house many people, can de discerned. Several three-sided rooms, known as *huairanas*, were built. This design allowed for a well-ventilated space for the storage of food. The *huairanas* had a pillar in place of their "absent wall", which would have held up the roof on that side. There are double *huairanas* where the rear wall forms a divide upon which a second *huairana* was raised on the opposite side. The roof, normally pitched, consisted of a frame made from tree trunks that served as a base for a protective covering of thatched *ichu* (*Calamagrostis spp., Stipa spp.*). The roof rested on two lateral walls, reaching to the triangular gable end. On the edges of the exterior wall stone keys were inserted for fixing the roof, and stone rings were used to secure the structure. The simple, three-walled single *huairanas* had just a

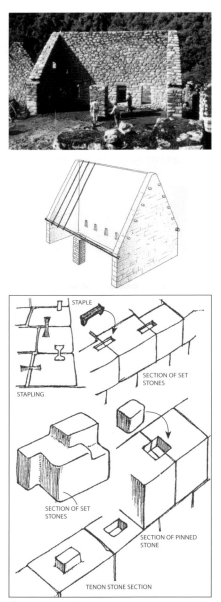

▲
A huairana, or three-walled building. Sometimes a pillar in the "missing wall" held up the roof. The roof was supported at the sides by gables or walls which reached the apex
Drawing: Gasparini and Margolies

▲
Illustration showing how metal elements were used in stone carving in Inca architecture
Drawings: Santiago Agurto

single pitched roof. In some cases, this roof was supported by a pillar raised at the centre of the "absent wall". The four-sided pitched roofs of other buildings, because they lacked gables, were held up by a frame of tree trunks resting on a ridge board.

In the case of the buildings with gables, the steep pitch of the roofs allowed for a well-ventilated attic space ideal for the storage of large quantities of food-stuffs. To this day, in highland villages, this space is used as a granary, or *colca* (koilka) in Quechua. At Machu Picchu these spaces must also have served for food storage. Access was via a ladder leaned against one of the sides of the hole made in the ceiling. In keeping with the typical pattern of Inca build-ing, the doorways at Machu Picchu are trapezoidal and are often double-jamb. The niches set into the interior, and occasionally exterior, walls are also trapezoidal. They may have been used as altars, for the placing of sacred ob-jects or even mummies. Windows are uncommon, but those that do exist are also trapezoidal.

Some doorways, such as the one giv-ing access to the Sacred Sector, on the southern side of the complex, may have been barred on the inside by a framework of trunks. The door, lack-ing hinges, would have been tied to a carved ring in one of the ashlars above and in the middle of the lintel. In addi-tion, it would have been tied laterally to two cylindrical stone supports on either side of the doorway.

For building material, the prefer-ence was for ashlars of white granite.

At Machu Picchu, the blocks were dragged from nearby quarries to the building site. Generally, the tech-nique employed for transporting the blocks consisted of dragging them, hauling them with ropes and sliding them along pathways covered with moistened clay. To cut the blocks, stone sledgehammers were used, and where possible natural cracks in the rock were exploited. [*]

Typically, the ashlars at Machu Pic-chu were cut and polished with great care, although there are also walls built with less care and with a dif-ferent finish. In his study of the vari-ety of Inca building styles, Santiago Agurto (1986) analyses the contri-bution of Jean-Pierre Protzen (1983) and judges that this author gives "the impression that practically all Inca walls were similar in design, that is, they were built from rectangular blocks placed in horizontal courses". And he adds: "... the designs were many, and so different that the carv-ing techniques applied to some could not be applied to others. Such is the case of those ashlars with recessed or internal angles, where the carv-ing process and the tools used were, without doubt, not those described by Protzen" (Agurto 1986).

The finely-joined stonework is built from regular blocks of a similar size or

(*) The hewing of the stone was not accor-ding to the pattern exhibited by a rock at Ma-chu Picchu. This stone was prepared just a few decades ago, as an experiment, to show that at Machu Picchu a process similar to that emplo-yed by the Egyptians to cut stone might have been used.

from polygonal blocks. However, the walls not only differ in the cutting of their ashlars but also in their size. There are also perceptible variations within a single structure. One of the unique aspects of Inca building techniques present at Machu Picchu are the ashlars moulded to the form of the living rock. The exquisitely wrought ashlar walls were carefully worked not just on their visible surfaces and angles, but also at the sides. Each stone fits perfectly with its neighbours. Often a wall consisted of two parallel walls, finely-wrought, with the space in the middle filled with rubble and mud. In common with Inca architecture in general, the walls at Machu Picchu are not vertical, but rather inclined.

The walls are remarkably stable, due to the careful assembly of the ashlars, their inclined design, and also because their bases are set deep into the earth, as evidenced by the excavations carried out by Elva Torres in the Prison Sector (Wright and Valencia 2001, p.92, fig.119). The retaining walls of platforms usually have drainage systems.

An important tool for the stonemason was the diorite hammer, or one fashioned from a meteoritic rock, *jihuaya*, which is exceptionally hard. It "has been demonstrated that the Incas also used chisels made from tempered copper or bronze with a high tin content" (Agurto 1987). Agurto believes that "without such tools it would have been impossible to make the join between the mortise and the tenon, for example, or in the setting of two stones" (Agurto 1986). The final

Different architectural characteristics:

(1) The roof structure, which was covered with straw (ichu): (a) How the roof was supported by stone keys. (b) Stone rings set into the gables to support the roof
Illustrations: (1) Hiram Bingham; (a) Gasparini and Margolies; (b) Photo Kauffmann Doig)

(2) Diagrams of Inca architecture in general
After Graciano Gasparini and Luise Margolies)

(3) The trapezoidal form of doorways, windows and niches characteristic of Inca architecture: (a) Window, (b) Double-jamb doorway, (c) Niche or blocked-off doorway

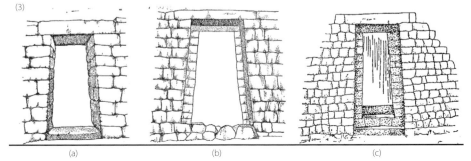

(a)	(b)	(c)

polishing of the ashlars was achieved through abrasion, using wet sand. Occasionally, the stone walls were plastered with mud and painted red or in other colours (Gibaja 2001). The astonishing perfection of the cutting and polishing of the ashlars can best be appreciated on the north wall of the Temple of the Three Windows, or in one of the external walls at the rear of the Water God Shrine (Tower). In the Temple of the Three Windows, the polygonal stones have been gradually shifted from their original position by tectonic action, and the resulting cracks reveal the meticulous care with which the ashlars were cut and polished, even on the sides that were not visible, thereby allowing them to be perfectly fitted. The whole structure can be likened to a subtle jigsaw puzzle, and is unrivalled anywhere beyond the frontiers of the Inca empire. The urban plan of Machu Picchu, according to Manuel Chávez Ballón, was similar to that of Cuzco. For Fernando Cabieses (1983), the architecture at Machu Picchu sums up the "Andean" concept of the "three worlds", through the altars dedicated to the regions of *hanan* (above), *hurin* (below) and *cay* (here). Víctor Angles (1972) points out that the urban plan of the site evokes the figure of a bird with its wings outstretched, which according to Fernando E. Elorrieta Salazar and Edgar Elorrieta Salazar (1996), is a condor (*Vultur gryphus*). If this is indeed the case, then at Machu Picchu we are witnessing another example of urban iconographic design, as seen at Cuzco (Rowe 1987) and Chavín de Huantar (Kauffmann Doig 1985).

In order to explain the high degree of perfection in the carving and fitting of Inca stonework, the popular imagination has created the myth of *cacacllu* (kak-kaqliu). This legend claims that the secrets of the stone-masons' art will never be known because the *cacacllu* bird stole the masons' tongues to prevent them from teaching future generations. Another supernatural explanation for the delicate finishing of the ashlars tells of how the ancient Peruvians knew the secret of "kneading" the stone thanks to a solvent they extracted from an unknown plant. The myth goes on to tell of how men discovered the technique upon observing the way certain birds pecked at rock walls with leaves in their beaks to make the holes they nested in.

The need for agricultural terraces was dictated by the region's rugged topography, for no other type of farming is possible on such steep slopes. There are two types of terracing: those exclusively for cultivation and those designed to prevent landslides on steep, unstable slopes. Some terracing would have fulfilled both roles simultaneously.

(1)

(2)

(3)

Way of moving the stone, from a drawing by Guaman Poma (c.1600)

Two forms of stone used in Inca construction in general: (1) Ashlars arranged in horizontal courses. (2) Wall built from polygonal stones, usually of great size

One of the sixteen Pacchas or ceremonial fountains
Photo: Courtesy RUMBOS de Sol & Piedra

Chapter 9

Machu Picchu:
A Note on Agricultural Engineering

Prototypically, agricultural terraces consist of a wall built from irregular stones which sustains a platform. The wall was covered with ashlars, usually polygonal and carefully worked. The surface of the terraces was covered with fertile soil transported to the site. The terrace system prevented soil erosion caused by rainfall, as well as providing a level surface for the efficient growing of crops on steep slopes.

The research carried out by the Wright Water Engineers company of Denver, Colorado since 1994 has provided much information regarding the water supply and drainage system at Machu Picchu (Wright, Witt and Valencia 1997; Wright, Valencia and Lorah 1999; Wright and Valencia 2001). Water was collected from a spring located on the slopes of Machu Picchu hill and channelled by gravity along a 749 metre long canal capable of carrying 300 litres per minute. The spring not only supplied

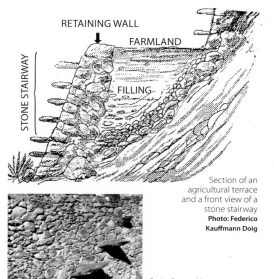

Section of an agricultural terrace and a front view of a stone stairway
Photo: Federico Kauffmann Doig

Stairs formed by stones embedded in the wall

the needs of the inhabitants of Machu Picchu, but also provided water for the worship of that element in the series of artificial waterfalls known as the Fountains, or *Pacchas* (paqtshia). The Wright research has established that the water system at Machu Picchu was not designed to irrigate the terraces, despite the fact that some of the channels flow through the terraces (Wright and Valencia 2001, pp.95-97, 103-109, Fig.121). Cultivation on the terraces was non-irrigated, and the main purpose of the Dry Moat would have been the collection and drainage of rainwater.

(1) One of the two stairways that run parallel to the wall on one side of the Sacred Sector. In the centre the Pacchas can be seen with their series of ritual pools. (2) One of the water channels that fed the Pacchas
Photos: Federico Kauffmann Doig and Willy Loayza

(1)

(2)

Separation of ashlars due to the
tectonic movement at the site
Photo: Federico Kauffmann Doig

Chapter 10

Machu Picchu:
and Soil Instability

Machu Picchu rests on a sector of Vil-cabamba batholith, a natural formation composed of intrusive rocks of great depth and different rock types, including grey white granite, tonalite and granodiorite.

According to the pioneering geomorphological studies of Carlos Kalafatovich (1963), the "geological chaos" upon which the monument of Machu Picchu and other neighbouring sites are built has left its mark on several of its sectors (Alegría 2001) For example,

according to Luis A. Pardo (1961a), the group of structures known as the Intihuatana would have collapsed if it had not been repaired in time. The multiple factors causing the deterioration of the site have been examined by V. Carlotto Caillaux and J. Cárdenas Roque (2001), R. Benavente Velásquez (2001) and J.F. Bouchard, V. Carlotto and P. Usselmann (1992). Their conclusions are based on geomorphic and geological considerations and observation of the damage caused to the architecture.

Alarming conclusions regarding the rapid displacement of the soils upon which Machu Picchu rests were published in 2001 by Kyoji Sassa, of the Institute of Research into the Prevention of Landslides, at the University of Kyoto, Japan. In his report, published in the magazine New Scientist, he calculated that the geodynamic displacement at Machu Picchu was up to one centimetre per month (Kauffmann-Doig 2001b). For Pablo Vidal Taype Ramos, this conclusion does not reflect the reality of the situation, because the Japanese scholar made his observations on the ground surface, at depths of between 0.5 and 3 to 5 metres. He maintains that calculations should not be based on that stratum, but instead on the geodynamics of the intrusive rocks upon which Machu Picchu rests. Carlos Necochea and Bernabé Calderón (2001) also agree that the "granite massif" upon which Machu Picchu rests prevents it from collapsing.

In common with the geologist Jaime Fernández in 1955, Kalafatovich concluded in 1963, after several years of research, that "the igneous intrusive rock is profusely fractured", leading to geological faults, water erosion and landslides. Experts from UNESCO have indicated that there exists a risk of serious displacement of large areas of subsoil at Machu Picchu as a result of geological faults of varying magnitude, although they point out that the movement is slow. Landslides were

observed in Inca times (Carlotto and Cárdenas 2001; Kalafatovich 1963).

These tectonic problems are evident in the deterioration suffered by some walls over time, for example at the Main Temple, the relatively slow advance of which can be seen in photos taken in 1912, when compared with the current condition of the structures (Vargas 2001)

Conservation of the walls faces another challenge: rainwater, especially on those walls unprotected by roofs.

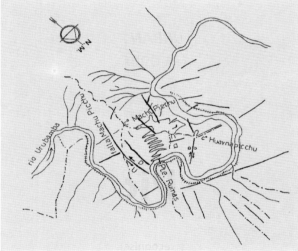

Geological faults

U→
D← Faults that show the position and arrangement of the blocks

U = raised block.
D = fallen block.

Map of the geodynamics of the soils in the Machu Picchu area
Ruperto Benavente Velásquez

Drawing showing the problems affecting the architecture at Machu Picchu and the lack of action on the part of the relevant authorities ("El Comercio" 24/12/1952). The caption reads:

Mr. Regional Inspector.

If the tower comes down the monument will fall

What are we waiting for? Until all this becomes a pile taken away by the wind?

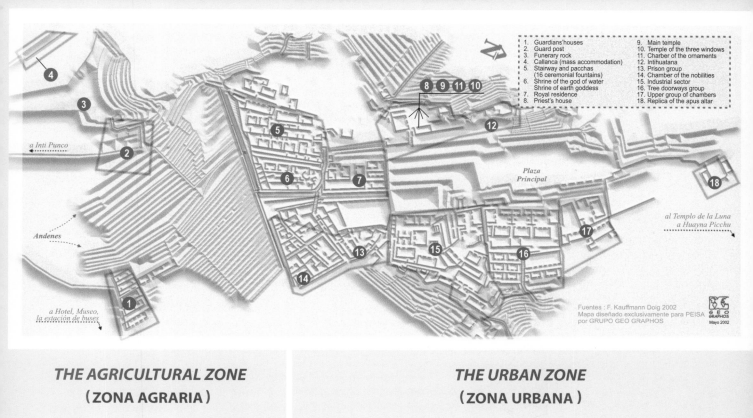

1.	Guardians'houses	9.	Main temple
2.	Guard post	10.	Temple of the three windows
3.	Funerary rock	11.	Charber of the ornaments
4.	Callanca (mass accommodation)	12.	Intihuatana
5.	Stairway and pacchas	13.	Prison group
	(16 ceremonial fountains)	14.	Chamber of the nobilities
6.	Shrine of the god of water	15.	Industrial sector
	Shrine of earth goddess	16.	Tree doorways group
7.	Royal residence	17.	Upper group of chambers
8.	Priest's house	18.	Replica of the apus altar

Fuentes : F. Kauffmann Doig 2002
Mapa diseñado exclusivamente para PEISA
por GRUPO GEO GRAPHOS

Mayo 2002

THE AGRICULTURAL ZONE
(ZONA AGRARIA)

THE URBAN ZONE
(ZONA URBANA)

Chapter 11

Description of Machu Picchu

Machu Picchu can be seen in all its splendour and magnitude from the pass known as the Intipuncu (Intipunku), situated one kilometre from the ruins[*]. From this almost aerial view the buildings appear to have been arranged across an irregular topography surrounded by rugged, high peaks. The scenery is characterised by the tropical vegetation typical of the Amazonian Andes, while in the distance, in contrast, white snow peaks rise against the horizon. Located 2,400 metres above sea level and at 13° 32' 23" LS and 72° 32' 34" LW, the architecture of Machu Picchu stretches for some 800 metres over a saddle between the peaks of Machu Picchu and Huayna Picchu.

In overview, Machu Picchu can be seen to be divided into two main areas, known as the Agricultural Zone and the Urban Zone, respectively comprising fields for crops and architectural structures. These structures can be further divided into two sectors, the Sacred Area and the Residential Area. Each of these contains groups of buildings with a varying number of chambers. The groups in both areas bear universally recognised names, usually those coined by Bingham. [**]

(*) At Intipuncu there are important remains that must have once been a kind of control point guarding the access routes to Machu Picchu, perhaps the main access.

(**) Several authors have described Machu Picchu in varying degrees of detail. In chronological order, we list some of them: Hiram Bingham (1930, 1948, 1949, pp.199-280), Humberto Vidal (1958, pp.189-200), Luis E. Valcárcel (1961, 1964), Hermann Buse (1961 and 1978), Juan Larrea (1961), Víctor Angles Vargas (1972), Luis Enrique Tord (1975), Fernando Cabieses (1983), Peter Frost (1989), Johan Reinhard (1991), Peter Frost et al. – Jim Bartle –Ed. 1995), Antonio Zapata Velasco (1999), Elena González and Rafael León (2001), Ruth M. Wright and Alfredo Valencia Zegarra (2001), Federico Kauffmann-Doig (2001a), Darwin Camacho Paredes (2004).

▶
A sector of the agricultural terraces of the Agricultural Zone at Machu Picchu. In the background are the so-called Guardians' Huts
Photo: Courtesy Wright Water Engineers, Denver Colorado / USA

(1) The so-called Watchman's Hut, in the Urban Sector
Photo: Courtesy Wright Water Engineers, Denver Colorado / USA

(2) The sculpture known as the Funerary Rock, in the Agricultural Sector
Photo: Hugh Thomson

(1)

(2)

THE AGRICULTURAL ZONE

This zone comprises agricultural terracing; successive stepped platforms set into the slopes of the rugged local topography (Cook 1916). The retaining walls of the terraces reach an average height of over four metres. Stone steps are set diagonally into the walls, giving access from one terrace to another.

Among the foods grown at Machu Picchu, maize (*Zea mays*), the most widely consumed food in ancient Peru, was the principal crop. Because Machu Picchu stands at 2,400 metres above sea level, coca (*Erythroxylon coca*) could not be grown, as it does not flourish at such altitudes.

We have shown that cultivation was non-irrigated (Wright, Kelly and Valencia 1997; Wright and Wright 1997). It is estimated that in Inca times annual rainfall was around 1,940 mm., contrasting with recent years, when rainfall has averaged 2,100 mm. (Wright and Valencia 2001, pp.103). The irregular rainfall average experienced today, which inevitably affects production negatively, would also have occurred in the past due to the El Niño phenomenon. Today, however, other factors have come into play, including the increase of carbon dioxide in the atmosphere, contributing to global warming. In the Amazonian Andes the seasons are limited to wet and dry, and the rainy season lasts from November to May.

In common with the terraces on the steep slopes of Huayna Picchu, those located on the edges of the Urban Zone at Machu Picchu were not principally used for the growing of crops. As we have already described, they were designed to prevent landslides.

The Agricultural Zone possesses a few buildings: the group known as the Caretakers' Houses, the Watchman's Hut and the *Callanca* (Kalianka) the largest structure. On the perimeter of the Agricultural Zone lies the so-called Funerary Rock, with its carved and polished planes, and the Upper Cemetery, to the east of the *Callanca*.

These terraces, like those of the neighbouring agricultural and ritual centre of Wiñay Wayna, were more than mere farmland. They were made beautifully to honour the Earth Goddess, *Pachamama*, the provider of sustenance. The stepped form of the terraces may have inspired the Andean step emblem. It is believed that this symbol, repeated in Andean iconography, was the sign of *Pachamama*, or Mother Earth, already present in ancient Peru more than 3000 years ago (Kauffmann-Doig 1991a. 2, pp.208, 209 / fig.4).

THE URBAN ZONE AND ITS TWO AREAS

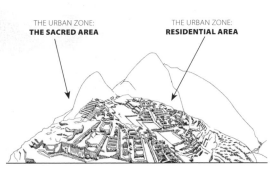

THE URBAN ZONE:
THE SACRED AREA

THE URBAN ZONE:
RESIDENTIAL AREA

The division between the Agricultural Zone and the Urban Zone is marked by the Dry Moat, which once served to drain rainwater.

The Urban Zone can be further divided into two large areas: the Sacred Area and the Residential Area. Both are separated by esplanades or plazas comprised of chambers and groups of buildings, including streets, stairways with a total of 3,000 steps and a system of lined water channels, some of which were used for the worship of water. The urban system has been described in detail by Ann Kendall (1974).

As already mentioned, the names of these groups are universally recognised and, in the main, were suggested by Bingham according to his own analysis of their purpose. In the case of the "Tower", or "Temple of the Sun", let us replace its conventional name with Water God Shrine, and in the case of the "Royal Tomb", we shall employ the term "Earth Goddess Shrine". We will justify these changes subsequently.

THE URBAN ZONE:

THE SACRED AREA

The Sacred Area is accessed via the doorway known as the City Gate. The Inca Trail descends to here, after passing the Intipuncu (Intipunku) on the high slopes of Machu Picchu hill. Among the many buildings of the Sacred Area the most noteworthy are: the Gateway Group, the Water God Shrine, the Earth Goddess Shrine (Royal Mausoleum), the Royal Residence, the Temple of the Three Windows, the Principal Temple and the Intihuatana, which occupies the highest part of the Sacred Area.

The Main or Principal Temple. A structure of the finest construction, its plan corresponds to that of a *huiarana*, or three-walled building. The central wall measures 11 metres. Behind and next to the Principal Temple is the Chamber of Ornaments, one of the stones of which has no less than 32 angles.

The Temple Of The Three Windows. Adjacent to the Principal Temple. Bingham believed at first that its three windows recalled the three caves of the mythical Tamputoco, metaphorically the vagina of Mother Earth, or *Pachamama*, from whence the ancestors of the Inca sovereigns emerged to found Cuzco. These are not windows for ventilation, but rather holes with a magical-religious significance lost to time.

The Water God Shrine (Tower, or Temple of the Sun). The ground plan of this structure would appear to recall the often repeated emblem of the Water God: the crest of a wave (Kauffmann-Doig 1991a, 2001b, 2001c). The floor, formed by a rock with a carved and polished surface, recalls the soils of Mother Earth, or *Pachamama*. It is the crest of a wave emblem which leads the author to believe that the Tower represents the Water God, and to rename it so.

The Earth Goddess Shrine. Traditionally known as the "Royal Mausoleum", this chamber is located beneath the rocky outcrop upon which stands the Water God Shrine, forming a cave. The rock walls of the interior of the Earth Goddess Shrine appear to have been veneered with carved, finely polished stones. Access to the cave is partially blocked by a stepped, stone sculpture comprising two parallel segments carved from the living rock and projecting from one corner of the wall of the cave near the entrance. The stepped nature of the sculpture may be a reference to the stepped terraces, but it would also seem to represent the stepped symbol of *Pachamama* (Kauffmann-Doig 1986a, 1991a, 2003b). Perhaps the cave also represents the vulva of *Pachamama*, the universal mother of the ancestors of all living things. According to the myths recorded by the chroniclers, humanity "burst from" several such caves.

The Royal Residence. This group is also known as the "Royal Palace". Although close to the shrines to Water

The Main Temple
Photo: Julio Corbacho

The Chamber of the Three Windows
Photo: Federico Kauffmann Doig

The Royal Residence with its successive doorways
Photo: Julio Corbacho

and Earth, it is separated from them by the *Central Stairway*.

The Pacchas (Fountains). Running parallel to the *Central Stairway*, the *Pacchas* are sixteen cascades clearly related to the worship of water.

The Intihuatana. The Intihuatana group is located at the highest part of the Urban Zone, which is the most important part of the Sacred Area and of Machu Picchu in general. Its remains rest on a rocky promontory reached via 70 steps. On the esplanade at the top stands an enormous sculpture carved from the living rock, with finely-wrought planes. Its perimeter is 8.60 metres and its height 1.76 metres. This enormous sculpture ends in a carved column known as the Intihuatana, 66 centimetres tall and cut horizontally at the top. We will detail in a separate chapter the possible function of this structure, which Bingham called the Intihuatana, based on a suggestive myth.

The stone sculpture known as the Intihuatana
Photo: Federico Kauffmann Doig

The Shrine of the Earth Goddess or Pachamama (Royal Tomb)
Photo: Federico Kauffmann Doig

► The Shrine of the Water God (Torreón or Temple of the Sun)
Photo: GHF Representaciones S.A./Lima

◀ General view of the
Residential Area
Photo: Federico Kauffmann Doig

▼ The Altar of the Replica of
the Apus
Photo: Federico Kauffmann Doig

THE URBAN ZONE:
RESIDENTIAL AREA

The Residential Area includes several groups of buildings: the Prison Group, the Mortar Building, the Three Doorways and the High Group, as well as the altar known as the Replica of the Apus, or the Sacred Rock.

Some of these groups may have been the dwellings of administrators, such as the officiating priests at ceremonies and, according to Bingham's suggestion, perhaps also of the *acclas*, or chosen women, who, among their other duties, would weave fine textiles, which had great diplomatic value for the Incas. In fact, the buildings of the Residential Zone, like those of the Sacred Area, although to a lesser degree, are rich in sacred meaning.

The Altar of The Replica of the *Apus*. Usually known as the "Sacred Rock", the Sanctuary of the Replica of the *Apus* is a stone resembling the silhouette of a group of mountain peaks charged with sacred meaning (Reinhard 1991, pp.54-55). This great sculpture is complemented by two *huairanas*, or three-walled structures (Valencia Zegarra 1977).

▶ Bird (of prey?) drinking from a vessel / Prison Group
Photo: Willy Loayza

▼ Two views of the Water Mirrors
Photo: Darwin Camacho Paredes

The Water Mirrors. Located in the so-called Industrial Neighbourhood, this is a group of constructions traditionally known as the "Mortar Group". The name derives from the presence, in one of the chambers, of a stone sculpture carved from one of the rocks in the floor of the building. This sculpture has two circular cavities of an obviously ritual significance, which Bingham interpreted as mortars. They may have been used for divination through the reflections made on clear water or other magical substances. That is why the author prefers to call them Water Mirrors, and to extend that name to the entire complex of buildings where they are found.

The Prisons. This set of constructions is adjacent to the Water Mirrors complex, although it stands below its neighbour. The walls contain niches of varying sizes and the damp narrow caves here are commonly believed to have been cells. An enormous rocky outcrop dominates the complex, and is partially covered with masonry on its upper part, which seems to represent the figure of a bird. The caves contain three niches, with space to accommodate a seated person. This has given rise to the theory that this was a jail. Devices in the walls would have served to tie the arms of prisoners. In one chamber of the Prison there is a rock with a carved figure. It is believed to portray a condor (*Vultur gryphus*), and does seem to have the characteristic ruff of this species around its neck. I believe, however, that it does not represent a condor, but rather a bird of prey drinking from a circular container. It should be remembered that a condor's ruff of feathers circles its entire neck, and not just its nape, as in this sculpture.

Stone Shrine. This is a pile of unworked stones, left exposed as a shrine to stone itself. Special powers are attributed to stones in Andean myth. They were believed to embody ancestors, for example in the story of the *purunaucas* told by Joan de Santa Cruz Yamqui Salcamayhua (1627 ?). In this story the stones are said to be warrior ancestors (*auca*), transformed from inert rocks into soldiers when called upon by the sovereign Pachacutec.

The Intihuatana sector occupies the highest part of the Urban Zone. This view shows the three-walled Main Temple in the foreground
Photo: Courtesy Heinz Plenge

The sculpture known as the Intihuatana together with a drawing by Guaman Poma (c.1600) showing a similar altar but crowned with a figure representing the Water God in human form. Observe also the clouds and heavy rainfall the figure has called upon through a llama sacrifice
Photo: Courtesy Giancarlo Ligabue

Chapter 12

The Intihuatana:
A Magical Means of Prolonging the Day?

As we have seen, at the top of the Sacred Area stands the complex known as the Intihuatana (Intiwatana). This most important of all shrines is crowned by a great sculpture carved from the rock outcrop, the surface of which has several carefully cut and polished planes. From this plinth there rises a prismatic pillar pointing skyward, and sculpted from the same stone that forms its base. This is the Intihuatana. It was Hiram Bingham who named this mysterious sculpture standing upright from its base. He chose to name it thus because of its similarity to a structure known as the Intihuatana at the ruins of Pisac, in the Urubamba valley, which was drawn – and captioned Intihuatana – by the traveller E. George Squier (1877). John H. Rowe (1946) has stressed the differences between the two stones, putting in doubt the accuracy of such a title for the stone at Machu Picchu. They are certainly not identical, but both do rise like columns from the living rock. *Intihuatana* is a Quechua word translated as "tying the sun", or "place where the sun is tied". Several theories purport to explain the purpose of such a sculpture. Basing themselves on its etymology and the reference to the sun (*inti*), several authors believe the Intihuatanas were astronomical devices (Zecenarro 2004). According to these scholars, they were solar observatories for predicting the solstices, particularly the winter solstice, which in the southern hemisphere falls on the 21st and 22nd of June. Those who have observed the shadows it forms as the day progresses suppose that the Intihuatana was a sundial. It should be pointed out, however, that for much of the year the sky above Machu Picchu is cloudy, which would make it less than ideal as an astronomical observatory. The author believes that if this was indeed its purpose, then that function would have been limited to predictions regarding agricultural production, which would place its role more in the realm of astrology than that of astronomy. Johan Reinhard (1991, pp.48-53) has made a detailed analysis of the so-called Intihuatana at Machu Picchu. His theory differs from those of his predecessors. He highlights the sculpture's relationship to the "sacred mountains" surrounding it. And, in addition to discussing the many conjectures made by Max Uhle (1910) regarding Intihuatanas, he proposes that the upright stone at Machu Picchu is a replica of a mountain, perhaps Huayna Picchu. Nevertheless, at the same time he does not rule out the possibility that the Intihuatana may have been used as an astronomical observatory to establish the equinoxes (Reinhard 1991, pp.48-50).

There may be a link between the stone *huancas* and upright sculptures like the Intihuatana. According to Ernst W. Middendorf (1990-92, 2, p.431), any "great single stone" was once known as a *huanca*. We have seen, especially in the Cordillera Negra, this name applied to long stones thrust into sown fields to make them fertile. They seem to represent the penis, which, upon penetrating Mother Earth or *Pachamama*, symbolically inseminates her. At Chucuito, the *huancas* clearly represent phalluses, and they were originally sited in sown fields (Kauffmann-Doig 2001c, 2002, v.6, p.965). The *huanca* tradition is an ancient one, for they are found at Caral, or Chupacigarro, in the Supe valley (Paul Kosok 1965; Ruth Shady 1997). John H. Rowe (1946) suspected that the word Intihuatana could be of recent provenance, stating that no reference is made to it in old dictionaries and it only appears for the first time in the 19th century, in an 1856 work by Clements R. Markham (Reinhard 1991, p.48). In fact, it was recorded much earlier, as "Yntiquatana" (Oricain; 1790, p.349). It may not have appeared in older dictionaries because it is in reality

composed of two terms, rather than a single word. Its Quechua provenance is beyond doubt. A drawing by Guaman Poma (c.1600, f.240) seems to show an *Intihuatana*, in the form of an altar, the pillar of which emerges from a flat base, as seen at Machu Picchu. As Max Uhle noted (1910) in the Cuzco region there exist other sculptures carved from the living rock and also known as *Intihuatanas*. The pre-Hispanic origin of the word appears beyond doubt. The word is used in a myth still told today and clearly of ancient origin, which seems to prove that the word Intihuatana was not coined by Squier (1877) or Markham (1856) or Oricain (1790). The myth tells of how ancient man was able to "tie the sun down" (*Intihuatana*).

As can be gathered from the myth, transcribed below, it was said that men could, through sorcery, "tie the sun down", thereby prolonging the daylight hours. The story says that this was done so that labourers would have more time to work in the fields and produce the foodstuffs essential to their existence (Kauffmann-Doig 2002, 4, pp.602-603).

The myth of "tying down the sun" persists, with minor variations, in parts of the departments of Apurímac and Cuzco. It is also included in one of the versions of the myth of Inkarrí, published by Alejandro Ortiz Rescaniere (1973). The passage tells of how Inkarrí "tied the sun so time would slow". Although this story does not specify why Inkarrí would wish for time to be slowed, it does demonstrate that it was believed the day could be prolonged by "tying down the sun". [*]

The version of the myth we transcribe here, in Quechua and in translation, confirms the pre-Hispanic antiquity of the word Intihuatana, as well as allowing us to propose a hypothesis regarding the purpose of these sculptures which differs from the usual theories. This version of the myth was recorded in the mid-20th century by Rubén Aucahuasi, in his native Apurímac. In 1979, when I asked him to transcribe myths from his native land, he kindly provided this story. One passage refers to the *Intihuatana* (Kauffmann-Doig 2002, 4, pp.602-603):

Clearly, this story tells of how, in ancient times, men were able to "tie down the sun". And it explains why they did so: to stay its course, in order to prolong the day and give the peasant more time to produce the crops that gave him sustenance.

Even if the upright stone at Machu Picchu known as the *Intihuatana* was not an altar used to "tie down the sun", myths like the one transcribed allow us to intuit the purpose of *Intihuatanas* in general. The story shows the urgency with which ancient Peruvians worked to produce enough food in the face of climatic phenomena such as El Niño, and how they had recourse to magic formulas to neutralise the recurring swings of fortune unleashed by the supernatural powers governing the elements (Kauffmann-Doig 1986a; 1991b; 2003b).

---

[*] There exists another myth that might offer a different version of the Intihuatana myth transcribed here. It was known to Bingham, and tells how the ancient Peruvians feared that the sun might one day stop shining, causing the end of the world. Perhaps these shrines were erected to avoid such a cataclysm by "tying down the sun"? It was thought that the sun could disappear during an eclipse. Garcilaso (1609, II, chapter XXIII) tells of how during eclipses the people gathered on the esplanades and begged aloud, to the accompaniment of fifes and drums, for the sun to survive this potentially fatal event. Garcilaso also says that during lunar eclipses the same ritual was performed, and part of the ritual consisted in the torturing of dogs so that their howls would be added to the pleas of their masters. The ritual survives, during eclipses, according to information gathered by the author in Cachora, Apurímac. But today pigs, rather than dogs, are whipped by their owners (José Quispe, Cachora, 1993).

Ñaupa runakunaqa, sinchi ñakarikuywansi kausayta tarisqaku

The men of ancient times made their living with great difficulty.

Monaraq achihaymanta, allin tuta yaykuykamas llank'asqaku.

From before dawn, until late at night, they worked.

Paykunapaqsi, p'unchauqa pisillaña kapusqa.

For them the day was too short.

Chaysi, pallay chumpikunawan INTITA WATASQAKU, sapay p'unchau llamk'ay usianankama.

That is why, it is said, THEY TIED DOWN THE SUN, with decorative ribbons each day until they finished their work.

Temple of the Moon (Sanctuary of the Pachamama)
Photo: Ruperto Márquez

Chapter 13

Around Machu Picchu

In the environs of Machu Picchu there are many other archaeological remains, such as those on the hill of Huayna Picchu, visible from Machu Picchu. The Temple of the Moon is also located nearby. Below we describe these sites in more detail:

Huayna Picchu. This is usually translated as "young peak", and is a rocky height standing some 400 metres above the Main Plaza of Machu Picchu. As we have already seen, the word *picchu* would seem to be a corruption of the Spanish word "pico", meaning the summit of a mountain. The Marquis of Wavrin (1961) climbed Huayna Picchu, accompanied by his guide Valdivia, and vividly described the adventure.

The constructions near the top of Huayna Picchu are reached by a path leading from Machu Picchu at the Replica of the Apus area, or Sacred Rock. A section of the path is formed by a steep staircase cut into the rock, which ascends almost vertically for more than 40 metres. The constructions on Huayna Picchu must have had an important religious significance. They consist of a doorway and a conglomeration of carved stones, which may have been part of a ruined or uncompleted shrine. There are many miniature terraces on Huayna Picchu. The limited surface area and the steep slopes seem to indicate that their function was the prevention of landslides.

◄
The Drawbridge
Photo: Courtesy Wright Water
Engineers, Denver Colorado / USA

Shrine to Pachamama, and comprise two octagonal chambers. The stones lining the cave were cut and polished with the greatest care and contain niches and blind double-jamb doorways. The site must have been an important place of worship, judging from the quality of the stonework. We call it the Shrine to Pachamama because it is a cave converted into a shrine. Caves may have symbolised the vulva of *Pachamama* or Mother Earth, from where according to myth the ancestors of the Incas emerged. A path leads from Machu Picchu directly to the Shrine of Pachamama, beginning near the Replica of the Apus, or Sacred Rock. Another path goes around the conical hill of Huayna Picchu and continues for another two kilometres.

The Drawbridge. The Drawbridge is situated some two kilometres from the gateway to the Sacred Area. The path follows a staircase that ascends alongside the *Callanca* and ends at the ancient Inca path. At the other end of the bridge the path continues on its course. On reaching the Drawbridge, and beyond it, the path narrows and continues along a kind of shelf set into the cliff face. The bridge was originally covered with logs which, when removed, prevented passage.

The Shrine To Pachamama (Temple Of The Moon). This site is located on the steep slopes falling away to the north of Huayna Picchu, some 400 metres below Machu Picchu, at 2,050 metres above sea level. Known to Bingham, who named it the "Great Cave", it was described in detail by Hermann Buse (1961) and Ann Kendall (1969). In 1997, Ernesto García Calderón and Roger Prada Honor cleaned a complex of buildings in another sector, discovered by Fernando Astete and Rúben Orellana in 1987. These are located close to the rock chamber lined with finely-carved stonework and known to us as the

Chapter 14
What Might Machu Picchu Have Been?
Diverse Opinions

There are many theories which try to explain what Machu Picchu was, beginning with those formulated by Bingham.

At first, on discovering a beautiful building with three large windows and known now as the Temple of the Three Windows, Bingham deduced that Machu Picchu must have been Tamputoco (Tanputoko), the mythical cradle of the Inca rulers. Without revising his initial opinion, he later began to believe that he may also have discovered what he had been seeking, Vilcabamba (Wilkapanpa) the Old, the final stronghold in the resistance to the Spanish invasion from 1536 to 1572 (Guillén 1994; Hemming 1970; Kubler 1947; Lee 1985, 2000; Lohman 1941, Regalado 1997; Vega 1964). Scholars now agree that Machu Picchu was neither Vilcabamba the Old nor Tamputoco. The former is located in Espiritupampa, and was located by explorations postdating those of Bingham (Savoy 1970; Lee 1985). Nevertheless, as we will see later, doubts remain regarding this hypothesis. The mythical site of Tamputoco lies south of Cuzco, in the vicinity of Pacarictambo (Bauer 1992, pp.41-63; Muelle 1945; Pardo 1946; Urton 1990).

Luis E. Valcárcel (1964, pp.88-91), believed that Machu Picchu was the historic Pitcos, which Baltasar de Ocampo Conejeros (c.1611) described as a place located "on a very high hill (…with) sumptuous buildings of great majesty (…)". His hypothesis

emphasises the similarity between the words *pitcos* and *picchu*, and stresses the high-flown description of Pitcos given by Ocampo, which seems to describe Machu Picchu. Valcárcel did not believe that Ocampo's Pitcos was in fact Vitcos, the fortified temple site in the Vilcabamba river basin, in Rosaspata, near the present-day village of Huancacalle, the geographical location of which is backed by precise historical references (Rodríguez de Figueroa 1565; Murúa c.1600; Calancha 1638).

Regarding the question of who lived at Machu Picchu, Bingham believed the majority of the inhabitants were women, based on an apparently high incidence of female remains among those found at the site. According to the first analysis of 135 sets of bones exhumed, 109 were female, 22 men and 4 children. Based on these preliminary findings, Bingham reasoned that they were *acllas*. In other words, Machu Picchu must have been a gigantic *acllawasi*, inhabited by chosen women dedicated to state tasks and prayer, and given as political gifts.

In their research, Richard Burger and Lucy Salazar-Burger (1993, p.24) had the benefit of revisions made in recent years to data regarding the bones recovered by Bingham, indicating that the ratio of male to female skeletons was in fact roughly equivalent - in common with the findings of Fernando Astete Victoria, who in 1994 discovered 18

skeletons in the eastern sector of the ruins, some 60% of which were adult males. Marino Sánchez Macedo (1990) still agrees with Bingham's original conclusions.

It is interesting to note that Ocampo Conejeros (c.1611) described Machu Picchu as an *acllawasi*, if Pitcos is indeed Machu Picchu, as Luis E. Valcárcel firmly believed. Ocampo describes Pitcos as a "fortress (…) on a very high hill, from where it dominates a great part of the province of Vilcabamba, with a most grand, flat plaza and sumptuous buildings of great majesty, skillfully constructed and all with lintels over their doors, both large and small, and beautifully sculpted from marble (…)". According to Ocampo, Tupac Amaru the First was raised in the Pitcos *acllawasi*.

The idea that Machu Picchu was a fortress designed to prevent incursions by Amazonian tribes is a theory Bingham himself rejected. The *Chunchos*, or forest dwellers, inhabit lower altitudes below 1000 metres above sea level. Machu Picchu's climate represented an insurmountable barrier for them. Strictly speaking, the word "citadel", in the sense of a fortified city, and often used to describe Machu Picchu, is inappropriate (Harth-terré 1961), for the site was not fortified. The Dry Moat, which separates the Urban and Agricultural Sectors, was merely a drainage ditch. Nor did the city's location or the walled sector on the edge of the site make Machu Picchu impregnable. The Intipunku would have controlled access to the city from Wiñay Wayna, but it cannot be said to have been a fortress. And even if it had been, against whom was it intended?

The subject of a close link between magical-religious practices and the majestic surroundings of Machu Picchu has been closely studied by the American anthropologist Johan Reinhard (1991, 2002), who reached valuable conclusions based on the following premise: "Machu Picchu can be better understood if the site is analysed in the context of the topography surrounding it, which was considered sacred". Reinhard details his theories regarding the magical character of the area's geography, which he interweaves with astronomical observations. There are many studies related to the astronomical character of the site, such as those of Raymond E. White and David S.P. Dearborn (1980), Katharina Schreiber, and Raymond E. White, which, supporting the Johan Reinhard thesis, place the site at the centre of a vast "sacred geography" and discuss the importance of the high peaks for the Incas, including Salcantay (6,271 metres). He also bases his conclusions on ethnographic data. It should be remembered that the high peaks were seen as "protectors and providers of economic stability". In other words, his studies underline the role of the *Apus*, or great mountains, where the Andean God of Water is still believed to reside. (Kauffmann-Doig 2002, 2003a and b).

A new hypothesis emerged when Luis Miguel Glave and María Isabel Remy (1983) revealed to the world a 17th century document featuring the name *Picho*, which they believe refers to Machu Picchu.

The authors (Glave and Remy 1983, p.191) demonstrate that in 1657 the Augustinians rented some lands known as Machu Picchu. John H. Rowe (1990) analysed the document of Glave and Remy, as well as older copies of the same document, and concluded that Machu Picchu formed part of an extensive estate "owned" by the sovereign Pachacutec.

The Rowe "royal hacienda" hypothesis, private property owned by the historical Inca sovereigns, has enjoyed the acceptance by many scholars, particularly in the United States. Susan A. Niles (2004) looks in detail at the concept of Machu Picchu as one of these royal estates, built by Pachacutec for his and his family's personal use. The author does not share this opinion, although it is endorsed by all scholars in the field, including researchers of the stature of Richard L. Burger and Lucy Salazar (2004; Burger and Salazar 2004; Salazar 2004b).

Regarding this controversial suggestion of the existence of private property in the Inca empire, other documents revealed previously by María Rostworowski (1963) and dating from the 16th century, are pertinent. In one, dated 1579, the Spaniard Gerónimo de Genares declares that since the time of the governor Lope García de Castro he had been the owner of the lands of Guaman Marca in the Amaybamba valley, and he mentions that these "belonged to the Inca Yupanqui who had them for his own recreation".

In the exegesis of such documents it is necessary to bear in mind that all the informants of the Spanish period, be they of mixed or indigenous blood, were forced to apply and adapt the Spanish vocabulary and the characteristics of

western institutions to the concepts and institutions of Andean culture, which were displaced almost from the very first moment of European irruption. For that reason, translations do not always reflect reality, for example in the case of the "possession" of land in pre-Hispanic times. It is likely that the references to "haciendas" refer simply to constructions ordered by a sovereign. In effect, with whom would Pachacutec have traded the produce of his "royal hacienda"? And what of Tupac Yupanqui, his successor and the "owner" of Chincheros? Or Huayna Capac, the "owner" of Yucay? The resources required by the state came from the two thirds of all food production paid in tribute by each family. These foodstuffs covered the necessities of the ruling class and public servants. Most of this tribute was stored for years of famine when recurrent periods of catastrophic weather conditions affected production. The preservation of the king's memory, the care of his mummy and the chambers he had inhabited were assumed by his *panaca*, or descendants. As the reader will have gathered, the author finds the conclusions drawn by Rostworowski (1963) and Glave and Remy (1983) implausible, for they imply that Pachacutec built Machu Picchu for his own recreation, a city which Rowe (1990) has described as having "buildings appropriate for the residence of a king and his court...". Such a conclusion begs the question: Did other administrative and religious complexes in the region of Vilcabamba, such as Wiñay Wayna, Phuyupatamarka or Patallakcta, also serve as private places of relaxation and leisure for the sovereign?

Chapter 15

A Different Hypothesis:

Machu Picchu as Part of a State Project for the Extension of the Agricultural Frontier

It would seem clear that Machu Picchu, in common with other archaeological sites nearby, such as Intipata and Wiñay Wayna, which have a similar design, was an administrative centre for food production and propitiatory rituals. We can also assume that only urgent necessity could have led a highland people to build places like Machu Picchu in the Amazonian Andes, a cloud forest region alien to them. As we will see, their motive was the urgent need to extend their agricultural frontiers. Nothing else could have persuaded the people of Cuzco to move to such an inhospitable region, where fieldwork required the additional task of forest clearance, an activity unknown in the highlands. The magnitude of such a project can be measured by the effort needed to erect the administrative and ritual centres needed to control agricultural production, as well as the terracing that tamed this rugged region. Such works could only have been accomplished within the context of a state program, the success of which only a sociopolitical structure as solid as that of the Inca state (or, previously, Tiahuanaco-Huari) could guarantee.

The labour required for such a project could only have come from the institution known as *mitmac*, under

Agricultural terraces built to extend the agricultural frontier at Machu Picchu and other neighbouring sites such as this at Wiñay Wayna
Photo: Courtesy Mylene d'Auriol

which entire peoples were transferred to other areas for political purposes. Chroniclers like Pedro Cieza de León (c.1550) tell how people were moved to unpopulated areas in order to increase food production. In a document from 1576, edited by María Rostworowski (1963, p.229), the informant had "seen and heard" that in the Amaybamba valley, near Machu Picchu, "in times past in that valley more than 1500 Indians lived… (and) all the Indians were *mitmaes*". The author adds that the people taken to Amaybamba "were *mitmaes* from all parts of the kingdom…", implying that they were highlanders and not Amazonian forest-dwellers.

The *mitmac* would have been controlled by Inca administrators. Engineers and stonemasons from Cuzco must have participated also, given the refined Inca style of the walls at Machu Picchu. The agricultural "colonization" project in Vilcabamba probably began with Pachacutec's time in the Vitcos valley around 1440, after his defeat of the Chancas (Cobo, c.1653, Book XII, chapter XII). The choice of the Vilcabamba region for the expansion of the agricultural frontier may have grown from its lack of population, particularly in areas such as Machu Picchu, where no evidence of pre-Inca inhabitants has been found. Also, the region is relatively close to Cuzco and, in the case of the Vitcos or Vilcabamba river basin, access was facilitated by the Urubamba river as it flows through Calca, Ollantaytambo, Amaybamba and Choquechaca. In Choquechaca, according to Bernabé Cobo (Cobo, c.1653, Book XII, chapter

XII), Pachacutec encountered hostile inhabitants, as well as in the Vitcos river basin and around the headwaters of the Pampacona river, "which is before entering the mountains" (i.e. the Amazon basin).

It should be reiterated that the process of colonization in the Vilcabamba region was overseen by the governors of the Inca state – administrators, priests and, of course, experts in the art of construction. Machu Picchu is one of many sites built in the region. The presence of extensive agricultural terracing, which covers the greater part of the site, as at Intipata and Wiñay Wayna for example, confirms that Machu Picchu's role was agricultural production. Whether or not the agricultural terracing was extensive enough to produce a surplus is another issue. Sites like Machu Picchu were also important centres of ritual worship, but the central role played by religion lay in supplying the magical assistance required for food production. To these motives for the Inca expansion into the Amazonian Andes, perhaps we should add the provision of coca (*Erythroxylon coca*); although coca did not flourish on Machu Picchu's terraces due to their altitude, it was possible to grow it nearby at lower altitudes.

Beyond the practical aspects of colonial expansion, we must ask a more fundamental question: Why expand the agricultural frontier? There can only be one answer: the increasing demand for food resulting from demographic pressure, due to the extreme scarcity of land suitable for agriculture in the ancestral lands of ancient Peruvian civilization.

This ecological imbalance can be traced to before the rise of the Inca state, some four thousand years ago, when ancient Peruvians began to plant crops and domesticate American members of the camel family (llamas and alpacas), abandoning the precarious existence of the hunter-gatherer. An agricultural economy provided a reliable food source, but at the same time it generated population growth and increased demand for food. To the challenge of limited land was added the El Niño phenomenon, which periodically interrupts production. Paradoxically, the recurrent natural disasters and the shortage of agricultural land which define Peruvian history at all stages of its development explain the growth of civilization through what Toynbee called the "response to challenge" (Kauffmann-Doig 1991b, 1996a).

The aim of agricultural colonization at places like Machu Picchu, Wiñay Wayna and Intipata was not limited to self-sufficiency, but rather to the production of a surplus that could be exported to other regions to cover periodic food shortages. Circumstance obliged the Andean people to provide for years of famine, and in the Inca state the peasant farmer was obliged to work his fields with optimum efficiency in order to produce the surplus necessary to meet the tax of two-thirds of yield demanded by the government. This tribute was required by the elite who managed the economy, but a far greater proportion was stored (Huaycochea 1994; Morris 1967) for redistribution during difficult times.

Corn was the principal crop, followed by potato. The earth was worked to produce an excess, to be stored for years when crops would fail due to the El Niño phenomenon. The main tool was a foot plough, or chaquitaclla, which is still used today

Traffic from Machu Picchu and the other administrative and religious centres of the region followed the trail from Machu Picchu to Patallacta (or Llactapata = laktapata) in the Cusichaca (Kusitshaka) river basin, and from there to Cuzco via Calca. Concerns over whether such a project might fail or, on the contrary, produce satisfactory results, were secondary to the prime objective: the initiation of a strategy to fight hunger. The study made by Alfredo Valencia and Arminda Gibaja (Frost et al. – J. Bartle (Ed.) 1995, p.23) of the yields Machu Picchu was capable of producing are not, it is true, encouraging. They calculate that yields would have barely sustained 55 people – far less than the estimated population of Machu Picchu itself, which may have been as many as 300 (Wright and Valencia 2001, p.98). Based on these figures, Ann Kendall (1974, p.130) concludes that "the population (of Machu Picchu) may have been partly or largely subsidized…" and she suggests that such a food subsidy may have been provided by the farming settlements at Patallacta, in Cusichaca. It should be remembered, however, that the agricultural terraces at Machu Picchu extend all around the site, and are

still covered in places by dense tropical vegetation, as shown by the work of Fernando Astete and Rubén Orellana (1988). If Valencia and Gibaja are right, then it may be that Machu Picchu was a production centre still undergoing its implementation stage.

Machu Picchu is not an isolated case of agricultural expansion. The vast "colonization" program in the Vilcabamba region produced other centres of farming and worship. Some have areas for crops much larger than their urban zones where administrative and religious personnel resided. Such is the case at Intipata, Wiñay Wayna, Vitcos and, especially, Patallacta-Quente (Pataiakta-Qente) in Cusichaca.

Emilio Harth-Terré supposed that Machu Picchu was conceived as a "self-sufficient city" (Harth-Terré 1961). But surely the objective of such a program would have been the production of a surplus? Such a supposition would tally with the calculations made by Ann Kendall in the Cusichaca area, which she maintains was capable of "feeding some 100,000 people a year", adding that Cusichaca produced four times more than it required to feed its inhabitants (Frost et al. J. Bartle (Ed) 1995, p.111).

Our theory regarding the presumed function of Machu Picchu coincides with the opinion of Richard Burger and Lucy Salazar-Burger (1993, p.21), who maintain that Machu Picchu "can only be properly understood in the larger context of Inca social, economic and political structure". But to this should be added the role played by the city in a magical-religious context, perhaps making it more important than the other power centres linked to the control and management of agricultural production and corresponding rituals. Although we do not know the details of such religious practices, their obvious aim was to ensure a growing – or, at least, stable – level of food production. Ceremonial worship was designed to propitiate, through magic, the supernatural powers upon whom the securing of food depended: the God of Water and the Earth Goddess, or *Pachamama*. The former was feared for his ability to bring disaster to humankind, which is why Andean iconography represents the God of Water with threatening fangs, often decapitating his victims. To this day, he is venerated in the form of the Andean peaks known as *Apus*. From ethno-historical informa-

The Andean Water God is portrayed in Moche art with the fanged mouth of a feline. It is often shown together with the mountains, or Apus
Photo: Federico Kauffmann Doig archive / Museo Nacional de Arqueología, Antropología e Historia del Perú

▶

The annual pilgrimage of Qollur Riti in Cuzco, although ostensibly a Christian festival, is a clear testimony to the continued cult of the Water God. The peaks of the Andes are snow-covered, and it is this water which feeds the lakes, and the clouds that form around the peaks produce rainfall
Photo: Gustavo Siles

tion, the images drawn by Guaman Poma (c.1600) and scenes depicted on the native *queros* of the 16th century, we can deduce that the sun was none other than a symbol or personification of the God of Water (Kauffmann-Doig 2003b, pp.56-57). On the other hand, the Earth Goddess, his feminine counterpart, was a passive deity who waited to be fertilized by the God of Water. The presence at Machu Picchu of both of these supernatural beings at the head of the Andean pantheon is expressed in buildings of great votive significance: the Water God Shrine (Temple of the Sun), the Shrine to the Earth Goddess,

or *Pachamama* (Royal Mausoleum) and, particularly, the altar known as the Intihuatana. In addition, the care with which the agricultural terraces were built can also be seen as homage to the Earth Goddess, embellishing and making fertile the land (Kauffmann-Doig 1986a, 1996a, 2001b, 2003a).

The colonizing urge must have been in evidence before the Incas, during the Tiahuanaco-Huari period, when some time in the 8th century highlanders occupied northern parts of the Amazonian Andes. However, in contrast with the events in Vilcabamba, these colonists gradually lost contact with their

Andean neighbours on the other side of the natural barrier formed by the Marañon river. This isolation modified their cultural knowledge and led to the creation of a *sui generis* Andean culture, that of the Chachapoyas (Kauffmann-Doig 1986a, 1986b; Kauffmann-Doig and Ligabue 2003).

The agricultural-ritual function we attribute to Machu Picchu can be seen in a much larger context - one that supposes all the monumental centres of ancient Peru were built for the same purpose, from the dawn of Peruvian civilization 4000 years ago; **vg. Caral, Mina Perdida, etc.**

The evacuation of Machu Picchu may have occurred during the resistance led by Manco Inca and his successors against Spanish rule, for Manco Inca recruited from the general populace of the Vilcabamba valley
Photos: Federico Kauffmann Doig; The Art Institute of Chicago / Richard F. Townsend

Chapter 16

Why
was Machu Picchu Abandoned?

With European irruption and the destruction of the socio-political structure and the power of the Inca state, Machu Picchu was probably abandoned due to its location in rugged territory difficult to reach. The evacuation of its inhabitants may have been brought about by the resistance to Spanish dominion led by Manco Inca and his successors from 1536 to 1572, who sought refuge in the Vilcabamba region, particularly in the river basins of the Vilcabamba or Vitcos and the Pampaconas-Concebidayoc. Manco Inca needed to recruit from the general population of the areas he passed. There is evidence to support this hypothesis. The inhabitants of Amaybamba were recruited by Manco Inca before he crossed the Urubamba via the Chuquichaca (Tshukitshaka) bridge on his way to Vilcabamba. A document from 1579, published by María Rostworowski (1963, p.229), refers to this evacuation, describing how the area was depopulated when the people followed Manco Inca on his way to Vilcabamba or Vitcos. The document says that "there were more than 1500 Indians in that valley (…) of whom (around 1579) only 57 remain". It should be added, however, that part of the populace, like the *mitmaq* of Chachapoyas, had long since been removed from their homeland, possibly on the orders of the Inca Tupac Yupanqui.

Even earlier documentary evidence backs the hypothesis that the population of Machu Picchu was recruited by Manco Inca. Rodríguez de Figueroa (1565) was charged with the mission of persuading Titu Cusi Yupanqui, Manco Inca's successor, to submit himself to Spanish rule. The Spaniard writes that on passing Condormarca, on his way from Amaybamba, "three leagues from the land of the Inca", he noticed that the place "was depopulated, because all have hidden in those mountains (of Vilcabamba)".

The abandonment of Machu Picchu, as opposed to that of Amaybamba, was probably not total, as evidence of European manufacture attests (Bingham 1949, p.264). Bingham excavated a bovine bone and two peach seeds, of obvious Spanish origin. Based on reports by George F. Eaton, Bingham adds that he also found "a fragment of a bovine tibia". To such findings can be added cultural objects of European origin, such as shards of glass and post-Inca pottery (Manuel Chávez Ballón / personal information 1964). Other remains not of late colonial manufacture may be supposed to have been introduced to Machu Picchu at a later date. To the findings mentioned should be added, perhaps, the 555 mysterious discoid objects found by Bingham, if in fact they are not, as some believe, poor copies of Spanish coins. For 400 years Machu Picchu was unknown to

all except local peasants and landowners. John H. Rowe (1990) highlights an old reference to *Picho* – which he supposes corresponds to Machu Picchu. In his chronicle, Diego Rodríguez de Figueroa (1565, p.94), writes that on the road from Cuzco to Vilcabamba in the village of Condormarca "there was a bridge in ancient times that crossed the Vitcos river on the way to Tambo and Sayacmarca and Picho…". Rowe checked copies of the 16th century manuscript in the Cuzco Departmental Archives, which had been mentioned previously by Luis Glave and María Isabel Remy (1983) in their monumental and methodical research. These documents mention *Picho* or *Picchu*, referring to the geographical area rather than to any constructions. Another 16th century document found by John H. Rowe (1990) refers generically to "a list of the agricultural lands in the Picchu canyon". For his part, Rafael Varón Gabai (1993) has found in a document from 1550, kept in the General Archive of the Indies in Seville, another mention of Picchu. The document refers to the tribute paid by the natives. Another document found by Varón, dated 1560, makes reference to an inspection or "visit" made of *Picho* by Damián de la Bandera. The document fixes a tax payable exclusively in coca. As coca was unsuited to the terraces at Machu Picchu, the inhabitants of this *Picho*, if it was indeed Machu Picchu, must have cultivated it in the surrounding valleys, at altitudes of less than 1000 metres. The landowners of the 16th century knew that the heights

above the Urubamba valley where Machu Picchu is located were unsuitable for agriculture. Varón (1993) points this out, citing documents discovered in the early 1990s. The difficult access to the terraces at Machu Picchu and neighbouring sites such as Phuyupatamarca, in the absence of the state structure of the Incas, meant that it was now impossible to control and collect state taxes in the area. And it is symptomatic of this situation that in 1911, the year of the scientific discovery of the ruins, then part of the Cutija hacienda, only two families lived at what is today the most celebrated archaeological site in Peru. Another early mention of the names Machu Picchu and Huayna Picchu appears in a 1782 document transcribed by José Uriel García (1961a, p.177 / Kendall 1974, p.134). But it does not refer to the ruins, but rather to some lands "without farm implements, livestock or houses".

Clearly, Machu Picchu was never totally forgotten. A few 19th century travellers and explorers heard about the ruins and made minimal references to the site in their drawings and maps (Gohring 1877; Wiener 1880). And when, in 1911, Bingham climbed its heights, captivated by the vision before him, members of two humble families came out to meet him.

As has happened with so many other vestiges of a great past, the ruins of Machu Picchu were locally known long before an enthusiastic foreigner like Hiram Bingham arrived to marvel at them. And a century later, it might almost be described as puerile xenophobia or at the very least simple pettiness to deny that it was through Bingham that this incredible marvel of Peruvian architecture was revealed to the world.

Huamanmarca or Guaman Marca. One of the doorways being repaired. The site was evacuated when Manco Inca withdrew from the Vilcabamba region. The inhabitants, willingly or forced, followed him, swelling the ranks of the neo-Inca army

The Inca Trail to Machu Picchu
and the Monuments it Links

A vast network of roads crisscrossed the land of the Incas. John Hyslop (1992), calculated that in total the system covered more than 23,000 kilometres. It crossed desert and mountain, and the Spanish chronicler Piedro Cieza de León (1553) commented with astonishment that the Inca roads were "made with great difficulty in that harsh and impenetrable land, and provoke admiration". The roads were partly built over routes already established before the rise of the Inca state. The Inca road system was known as the *Inka Ñan* (Inka Niam) or *Qhapaq Ñan* ("Royal Road"). The main highways were reserved for the state and not open to the general populace, and at bridges travellers were strictly controlled. The populations in the vicinity were obliged to maintain the roads in good condition. Today, the Inca Trail to Machu Picchu begins at Qorihuayrachina, an archaeological site located at Kilometre 88 of the railway line from Cuzco to Machu Picchu. It is also possible to begin the trail at Piscacucho at Kilometre 82, or Chilca at Kilometre 77, reached by the present-day road.

Another access route to Machu Picchu was discovered by Fernando Astete in July 1995. This route, clearly of Inca construction, had been buried by a landslide long ago. Astete states that this and other paths led to Machu Picchu via the

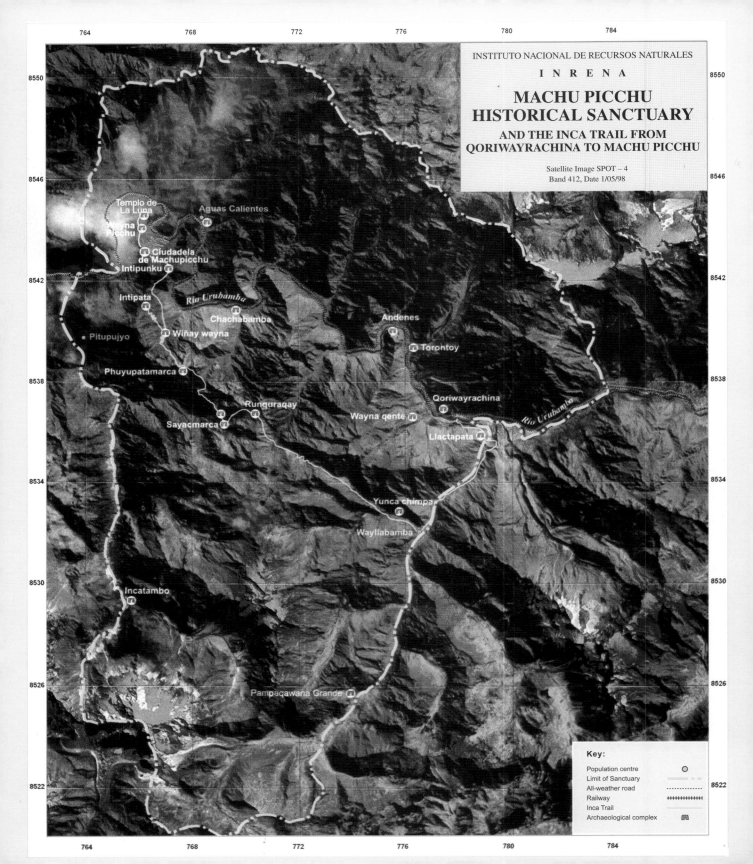

INSTITUTO NACIONAL DE RECURSOS NATURALES

I N R E N A

MACHU PICCHU HISTORICAL SANCTUARY

AND THE INCA TRAIL FROM QORIWAYRACHINA TO MACHU PICCHU

Satellite Image SPOT – 4
Band 412, Date 1/05/98

Key:

Population centre	○
Limit of Sanctuary	
All-weather road	
Railway	+++++++++
Inca Trail	
Archaeological complex	⌂

Templo de La Luna
Wayna Picchu
Aguas Calientes
Ciudadela de Machupicchu
Intipunku
Intipata
Río Urubamba
Chachabamba
Pitupujyo
Wiñay wayna
Andenes
Torontoy
Phuyupatamarca
Qoriwayrachina
Runguraqay
Wayna qente
Sayacmarca
Río Urubamba
Llactapata
Yunca chimpa
Wayllabamba
Incatambo
Pampaqawana Grande

Other Access Routes to Machu Picchu

A network of roads in the Vilcabamba-Urubamba region linked agricultural-architectural centres such as Machu Picchu. As well as the "classic" access route to this splendid site preferred by, and marketed to, tourists, which leaves from Qoriwayrachina and has already been described in detail, other ancient highways are still used today and have been partially restored or adapted to modern use.

In addition to the routes already mentioned, beginning at Choquesuysuy and Chachabamba, which present few difficulties to travellers, the first years of this century have seen new opportunities emerge for the adventure traveller wanting to access Machu Picchu from a number of other places, including the ancient roads from Choquequirao, Huancacalle and Mollepata.

Inca Trail from Choquequirao to Machu Picchu . Courtesy: RUMBOS DE SOL Y PIEDRA

Inca Trail from Choquequirao to Machu Picchu

This route has been used by adventure travellers since 2002, when restoration work at the magnificent archaeological site of Choquequirao began. Choquequirao is located in what was once the territory of the "Incas of Vilcabamba", high above the right bank of the Apurímac River. From this region, during the second third of the 16th century, the neo-Incas attacked the Spanish forces that launched incursions from Cuzco and Huamanga (Ayacucho) (See Appendix "C").

RUMBOS DE SOL Y PIEDRA, a magazine featuring the cultural and natural marvels of Peru through good reporting and excellent photography, and owned by Mariela Goyenechea, organised and undertook an expedition along the route from Choquequirao to Machu Picchu (Velarde y Hupiu 2005). The RUMBOS team left Cuzco on the road to Abancay, passing Anta, Limatambo, Curahuasi and Saywite, before taking the dirt road that leads to the village of Cachora, from where they trekked to Choquequirao.

From the main square of Cachora (3,050 metres above sea level), the trail leads to the Choquequirao Pass (3,270 metres). From here the trail descends via Rio Blanco to an average altitude of 1800 metres, before climbing again to the campsite at Maizal (2,850 metres), 25 kilometres from Choquequirao. From Maizal the route climbs once more to the Victoria Mines (3,800 metres), an old copper and tin mine that once belonged to the Romainville family. After reaching the San Juan Pass (4,177 metres), the trail descends to the small village of Yanama (3,520 metres), situated 18.8 kilometres from Maizal. Condors are often seen along this stretch of the trail. From the Yanama Pass (4,690 metres), the imposing peak of Mount Salkantay (Salqantai) can be seen. From the Yanama Pass the trail descends to Totora (3,400 metres), another small village, and a good place to camp. From Totora to the next hamlet of Colcapampa (2,870 metres), with its thermal springs, is an eight kilometre walk. From here it is a further 12.5 kilometres to Sahuayaco Beach (2,140 metres), where it is possible to camp and access the road, along which it is a forty-minute drive to Santa Teresa, just a short journey from Machu Picchu.

Inca Trail from Huancacalle to Machu Picchu

An extensive network of Inca highways ran through the domain of the "Incas of Vilcabamba", the neo-Incas who kept the Spanish in check from 1536 until 1572 (See Appendix "C"). One of the alternative routes for adventure travellers wishing to access Machu Picchu is the route that follows stretches of the old Inca highway from Huancacalle to Santa Teresa, not far from Machu Picchu itself. This route has been trekked by the Peruvian journalist Alvaro Rocha (2004, pp. 54-55).

Huancacalle is situated on the left bank of the Vilcabamba River, and is reached from Cuzco via the road to Quillabamba, travelling through an imposing landscape dominated by peaks like Mount Veronica/Waqaiwillka ("sacred tears"in Quechua). The road descends to Chaullay, from where a road leads to Huancacalle, following the course of the Vilcabamba River, which drains at Chaullay. The route to Huancacalle passes through picturesque villages such as Lucma. Close to Huancacalle stands the archaeological site of Vitcos- Ñustaispana, which comprises the Inca's Residence, the imposing shrine of Ñustaispana and majestic agricultural terraces (See Appendix "C"). In Huancacalle there is a comfortable hostel (Six Manco), thanks to Vincent Lee, the great explorer of the Vilcabamba region. The hostel is run by the Cobos family, whose patriarch is a valuable source of information, having accompanied Lee on several expeditions.

From Huancacalle several ancient highways depart. One leads to Espiritupampa, while another heads for Choquequirao. The Huancacalle to Machu Picchu route is a continuous climb in an easterly direction to the village of Yanatile and on to Santa Teresa, two villages close to the Urubamba River and Machu Picchu). These communities are linked by a road. The route from Huancacalle to Machu Picchu borders Mount Sacsarayoc (5,936 metres). Alvaro Rocha points out that the trail took him as far as the Asuntina Pass, "taking us to the Racachaca River and the village of the same name, which the INC has established as the final stage, for now, of its work to recover this pre-Hispanic road system. But, clearly, the Inca highway does not end here, as we were later able to see for ourselves".

Inca Trail from Mollepata to Machu Picchu

To Santa Teresa and thence to Machu Picchu, this route also follows another stretch of Inca highway, which leaves from Mollepata and is also being discovered now by backpackers. Mollepata (3,875 metres) is located in the province of Anta, close to Limatambo in the Apurímac river basin. This route to Machu Picchu runs from south to north.

Inca Trail: Choquequirao – Machu Picchu

Inca Trail: Huancacalle – Machu Picchu

◄ A section of the Inca Trail to Machu Picchu
Photo: Courtesy PromPerú

The 20 metre long tunnel between Sayaqmarka and ▲
Phuyupatamarka, at 3800 metres above sea level
Drawing by Paul Fejos

left bank of the Urubamba river. The path discovered by Astete begins at Kilometre 104 of the Cuzco-Machu Picchu railway, before the Machu Picchu station, near the ruins of Chachabamba. It passes the ruins of Wiñay Wayna before joining the Inca Trail from Qoriwayrachina to Machu Picchu. The Chachabamba route covers some twenty punishing kilometres, climbing steps cut into the almost vertical rock. A 37 metre footbridge, built by Sonia Guzmán, crosses the Urubamba-Vilcanota river, where an Inca suspension bridge would have originally stood. Another trail, which leads from Choquesuysuy (Tshoqesuisui) to Machu Picchu, via Wiñay Wayna, discovered and travelled for the first time by José Koechlin, will be mentioned later.

From Qoriwayrachina, the hike to Machu Picchu is made in three or four days, overnighting at established campsites. On the way, three passes must be crossed: Warmiwañusqa (4200 metres above sea level), Runkuraqay or Runturaqai-i

(3950 metres) and a third just before descending to Phuyupatamarka (Phuiupatamarka). On this route a 20 metre-long tunnel leads to Sayakmarka (Saiakmarka) and Phuyupatamarka. The road allows walkers to admire the structure of Inca highways and, in addition to the thrill of using such a road, visit the archaeological sites along the route, such as Wiñay Wayna and Phuyupatamarka, which rival Machu Picchu as testaments to the colonizing efforts of the Incas in the Amazonian Andes. Travellers will enjoy beautiful scenery, amid exotic tropical flora and the snow-capped peaks that dominate the horizon, such as Salkantay (6271 metres), Pumasillo (6010 metres) and, in the distance, Verónica / Huaquaiwilca (5700

metres), all of which can be seen from the archaeological site of Phuyupatamarka.[*] The Inca Trail of which we speak and the majority of the monuments it links were brought to light by Hiram Bingham, who walked the route as far as Sayakmarka in 1915. Many years later they were more rigorously explored by Paul Fejos (1944), and Julio C. Tello and Manuel Chávez Ballón in the area around Wiñay Wayna. In 1985, Leoncio Vera Herrera (2001) located the complex of Kantupata. The Inca Trail and its archaeological sites have been meticulously described by Víctor Angles (1972, pp.335-380). Peter Frost (1989) has written a very practical description of the

DISTANCES (VÍCTOR ANGLES)

- From Qoriwayrachina to Kusichaka	3 km
- From Kusichaka to Wayllabamba	8 km
- From Wayllabamba to Warmiwañuska	10 km
- From Warmiwañuska to Runturaqay	5 km
- From Runturaqay to Sayakmarka	6 km
- From Sayakmarka to Phuyupatamarka	5 km
- From Phuyupatamarka to Wiñay Wayna	3 km
- From Wiñay Wayna to Machu Picchu	5 km
Total:	**45 km**

(*) According to statistics from the National Institute of Culture (INRENA 1999, p.233), while in 1984 6,263 visitors walked the Inca Trail, in 1997 266,033 hikers made the trek. Numbers continued to grow, damaging a road which during the time of the Incas was restricted to a few travellers wearing sandals or barefoot. In response, the relevant authorities have established new regulations governing the carrying capacity of the trail and protecting the almost virgin ecosystem through which it passes.

(1) The ruins of Qoriwayrachina, at the start of the traditional Inca Trail to Machu Picchu / **Photo: Gustavo Siles.** (2) Paucarcancha or Inkaraqay, ruins reached via a trail from Huayllabamba. (3) and (4) Ruins of Huayna Quente / **Photos: Gustavo Siles.** (5) Runkuraqay / **Photo: Ruperto Márquez.** (6) Sketch of an Inca suspension bridge

(1) Wiñay Wayna / **Photo: Ruperto Márquez.** (2) Phuyupatamarka in 1994 / **Photo: Ruperto Márquez.** (3) Sayaqmarca in 1995 / **Photo: Ruperto Márquez**

The plans are those of Paul Fejos: Wiñay Wayna (above), Phuyupatamarka (centre) and Sayakmarca

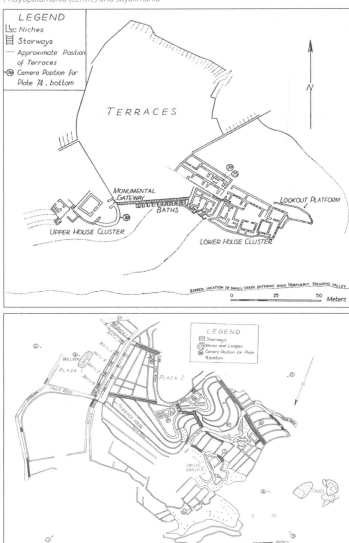

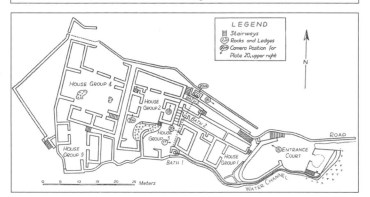

Patallacta, or Llactapata. Note the sinuous outer terraces, which may represent waves and be part of the ancient Peruvian worship of water.
Photo: Hugh Thomson

route. A more recent contribution is that of Rafael León et al (2000).

On the Qoriwayrachina-Machu Picchu route there are gruelling stretches, like the Warmiwañuska pass (4200 metres). The original Inca road, with steps carved into the rock, is only visible along certain stretches. Along the route a 20 metre long tunnel is negotiated. At Qoriwayrachina, the start of the Inca Trail, a bridge takes walkers across to the left bank of the Urubamba river. Here a cliff face has a staircase carved into it. Remains of the foundations of the original Inca suspension bridge still stand. The modern bridge was built by Ann Kendall's Cusichaca Project.

After crossing to the left bank of the Urubamba over the Qoriwayrachina bridge, the terraces of Quente (Qente), Machuquente and Waynaquente can be seen in the distance, among a grove of eucalyptus. At 3 km, before crossing the Cusichaca river, the enormous site of Patallacta appears, 2300 metres above sea level, in the triangle formed here by the Urubamba river. The group known as Patallacta also comprises the sites of Willcaraqay (Wilkaraqai-i), Pulpituyoc (Pulpitulioq),

Ruins of Huayllabamba
Photo: Gustavo Siles

Leoniyoc (Leoni-ioq) and Tunasmoco (Tunasmoqo), all in the Cusichaca area. These sites have been studied by Ann Kendall (1974, 1978 and 1988) and some of the terracing has been reactivated.

After crossing the Cusichaca, leaving Patallacta behind, the trail follows the river upstream along its right bank. Crossing the river again, the route leads to the Llulluchayoc (Liuliutshaioq) gorge and the village of Huayllabamba (Wailiapanpa), at 2500 metres above sea level. The walk from Qoriwayrachina to Huayllabamba takes approximately three hours, not including the time needed to visit the ruins of Patallacta and the other sites in the Cusichaca area. Huayllabamba is the only settlement on the Inca Trail to Machu Picchu. Its huts rest on archaeological remains, and stones from the ancient site have been used in their construction. [*]

It is from Huayllabamba that the original Inca road can be clearly distinguished. It travels uphill along the Llulluchayoc (Liuliutshaioq) river, which flows into the Cusichaca. The climb ends at the Huarmihuañusqa pass ("Where a Woman Died") at 4200 metres above sea level, the highest point of the route. From the pass there are fine views of Mount Verónica / Huacayhuilca or Waqaiwilka (5700 metres). Here there stands an *apacheta*, a pile of stones of different sizes. Following an ancient tradition, local travellers leave the stones as they pass by to thank the mountains for permitting them to make their journey without mishap.

Crossing the Huarmihuañusca (Warmiwaniusqa) pass, the trail abandons the headwaters of the Llulluchayoc (Liuliutshaioq) to descend to a swampy river

basin (3500 metres) that must be forded. The trail then climbs again, crossing the Pacamayo (Pakamaio) gorge and continuing to the ruins of Runcuracay (3800 metres). The journey from Huayllabamba to Runcuracay (Runkuraqai-i) takes about eight hours. Bingham found the name Runcuracay on a map, but he must have misunderstood what he read, for Víctor Angles calls the site Runturacay. *Runtu* means "round" in Quechua, which would describe the ground plan of the site. *Racay* (raqai-i) means "settlement".

The trail now climbs a slope to the second pass, at 4000 metres above sea level, before descending to the ruins of Sayacmarca (Saiaqmarka) at 3730 metres. This section takes a couple of hours.

Bingham visited these ruins in 1915. Whether or not the area was already known as Cedrobamba, this was the name he gave to the ruins. Sayacmarca, which means "inaccessible city", was named by Paul Fejos (1944). The ruins are reached along a seemingly interminable stairway cut into the rock. The

---

(*) From Huayllabamba an Inca road follows the course of the Cusichaca, called the Huayllabamba at this point. It heads in the direction of Pampacahuana (Panpaqawana), and leads to the ruins of Inkaraqay ("settlement of the Inca), known also as Paucarcancha after the village of the same name located nearby. Just before reaching Incaracay, the trail forks. One trail leads east and crosses the Silke river on its way to Ollantaytambo. The other leads to the Aobamba river at its confluence with the Urubamba west of Machu Picchu. On the way, at the mountain of Salcantay, this trail forks again and the new trail leads to the headwaters of the Santa Teresa and ends where the Huadquiña joins the Santa Teresa to flow into the Urubamba. These routes require stamina and the necessary logistics.

Choquesuysuy
Plan and drawings by Paul Fejos; Photo: Antonio Martínez

chambers at Sayacmarca are laid out in three groups set at different levels and crowning a rocky promontory. They were almost certainly related to the worship of rainfall or water. From Sayacmarca the trail continues to another set of ruins on the edge of Cedrobamba at 3570 metres above sea level. These ruins, two hours from Sayacmarca, are called Phuyupatamarka. From here the peaks of Salcantay (6180 metres) and Verónica or Waqaiwilka (5750 metres) can be seen. On the way to Phuyupatamarka a pass is crossed before the trail passes through a 20 metre long tunnel. Bingham explored these ruins in 1915, and called them Qoriwayrachina. Phuyupatamarka ("City in the Clouds") is the name given to the site by Paul Fejos (Fejos, 1944). Extensive agricultural terracing follows the sinuous topography and the shrines were dedicated to the worship of water. The stone is white granite. Between Sayacmarca and Phuyupatamarka the Inca road is impressively well-preserved, except for the final stretch, from whence several side trails are accessed.

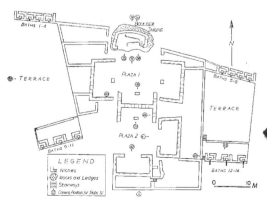

Plan of Chachabamba and details of the Chachabamba complex
Paul Fejos

The Intihuatana site, on the left bank of the Urubamba river (Km.121 of the railway) **Photo: Víctor Angles**

From Phuyupatamarka the trail descends from the cold high grasslands to a warmer climate covered with the tropical vegetation of the Amazonian Andes. In a couple of hours the ruins of Wiñay Wayna and Intipata are reached, and from there it is just a three hour walk to Machu Picchu.

One kilometre before Wiñay Wayna one passes the ruins of Intipata (2800 metres above sea level), with its 48 agricultural terraces divided by four stairways. Projecting stones set into the retaining walls provide access to the different levels. The highest part of Intipata boasts 23 small chambers. A road, unknown until 1983, links Phuyupatamarka with Intipata, facing the ruins of Wiñay Wayna. This is an alternative route discovered by the archaeologist Justo Torres in 1983-84. The Torres Trail, paved with slabs, is 5 kilometres long, has 3500 steps and is an average 2 metres wide. A tunnel provides rapid access to the trail's two levels, first up a series of 28 steps and then, after a rest, another series of 32 steps. Of particular interest along this route are the spiral steps carved into the rocky promontory. Percy Ardiles and Wilbert San Román restored this alternative route in 1986 (Ardiles 1990).

In 2001, in the area between Phuyupatamarka and Wiñay Wayna and the route described above, Leoncio Vera came across a site he named Kantupata (3370 metres above sea level). The site comprises chambers and terracing "the magnitude of which had gone unrecognised".

Julio C. Tello explored the ruins of Wiñay Wayna (2630 metres above sea level) in 1941. Wiñay Wayna (Winiai Waina) means "forever young", and is derived from the local orchids of the same name (*Epiden-*

drum secundum), found up to 3000 metres above sea level. The archaeological site includes groups of buildings and extensive terracing.

Wiñay Wayna is 5 kilometres from Machu Picchu. Halfway along this section of the trail stands the Intipunku, controlling access to Machu Picchu. From here a trail leads to the top of Machu Picchu hill, which without a doubt was once a place of worship. From Intipunku one descends to Machu Picchu, and the city can be seen in all its majesty from this point. Several trails originate at Machu Picchu. One climbs Huayna Picchu, while others lead to the Temple of the Moon and the Drawbridge. Another road descends to the banks of the Urubamba, and was discovered in 1998-99 by researchers from the Wright Water Engineers company (Wright, Valencia and Crowley 2000). In the vicinity of Machu Picchu other Inca roads link important archaeological sites lower down, close to the Urubamba river, such as Intihuatana (Intiwatana). Other sites, such as Chachabamba (Tshatshapanpa), Salapunku and Choquesuysuy (Tshoqesuisui), were accessed via Ollantaytambo, following the course of the Urubamba. From Chachabamba there is also a route to Salapunku and from there to other archaeological remains located in the area of Torontoy on the right bank of the Vilcanota-Urubamba.

The path to the ruins of Choquesuysuy and Wiñay Wayna is rough. Although it was discovered in 1991, it was walked for the first time in 1997 by its discoverer José Koechlin von Stein, together with the other hardy explorers who accompanied him. The Koechlin Trail is usually known as the

"Purification Path", due to the presence of large circular constructions known as pacchas (p'aqtsas) built at ground level in the lower sector of Choquesuysuy which must have once held water and been used for the worship of water.

The archaeological site of Choquesuysuy was revealed by Hiram Bingham and explored by the Fejos expedition (1944). It is located on the left bank of the Urubamba at Km.107 of the Machu Picchu railway.

The archaeological site of Choquesuysuy was revealed by Hiram Bingham and the Paul Fejos expedition explored the site (1944). It is located on the left bank of the Urubamba, at Kilometre 107 of the railway line to Machu Picchu. Beside a group of buildings there is a fountain divided into five segments, clearly designed for the worship of water.

Fejos also investigated the Chachabamba site, like Choquesuysuy on the left bank and almost on the edge of the Urubamba, at Kilometre 104 of the railway. Here walls rise resembling a bird with its head formed by and emerging from a great rock, not the first time we have come across iconographic Inca architecture (Kauffmann-Doig 1985).

The ruins of Salapunku form part of the Torontoy complex, which in contrast to the other sites described, is located on the right bank of the river, between Kilometres 80 and 100 of the railway line. Salapunku, at Kilometre 83, where the Urubamba gorge narrows markedly, has several agricultural terraces built on very steep slopes. The monument itself consists of a walled platform, which in its zigzag design resembles Sacsahuaman, although much smaller in scale.

Gould's Jewel-front
(*Heliodoxa aurescens*)

Buff-tailed Sicklebill
(*Eutoxeres condamini*)

Green-tailed Trainbearer
(*Lesbia nuna*)

Discover more than sixteen species of
hummingbirds at the Machu Picchu Pueblo Hotel
Courtesy INKATERRA

■ **Appendix B**

Its Flora and Fauna
The Machu Picchu Historical Sanctuary

Geographically, Machu Picchu is partly located in the Andes and partly in the Amazon, and is characterized by tropical vegetation. This mixed region can be described as Amazonian Andean. The monument itself lies on the perimeter of the Machu Picchu Historical Sanctuary, declared a World Natural and Cultural Heritage Site by UNESCO, created in 1983 and covering an area of 32,592 hectares. As well as Machu Picchu, other imposing archaeological groups exist in the area, principally those linked by the Inca Trail that runs through the

Machu Picchu Historical Sanctuary between Qoriwayrachina and Machu Picchu. According to the experts Alfredo Valencia, Fernando Astete and Octavio Fernández, there are more than 150 archaeological sites in the Machu Picchu Historical Sanctuary (National Institute of Culture – Lima / National Institute of Culture – Cusco).

The invaluable archaeological heritage of the Machu Picchu Historical Sanctuary combines magnificently with the splendid natural surroundings that are the habitat of unique species of flora and fau-

na (Vargas Calderón 1961, 1992), some of them threatened with extinction.

The flora is luxuriant, particularly in the humid zones between 2000 and 4000 metres above sea level. In the highlands several species of high Andean grasses are found. In the lowlands enormous, ancient trees grow: alder (*Alnus jorullensis*), pisonay (*Erythrina falcata*), walnut (*Juglans neotropica*), intimpa (*Podocarpus glomeratus*), quisuar (*Buddleja incana*), queuña (*Polylepis racemosa*), cedar (*Cedrela sp.)* and other species cover the gorges and forested

Cóndor *(Vultur gryphus)*, a bird often
seen in the sky above Machu Picchu and
the surrounding area
Drawing: A. von Humboldt

Spectacled bear *(Tremarctos ornatus)*
Photo: Courtesy Walter Wust

◄

Beautiful example of Andean flora
Photo: Courtesy Atilio Caipani Gutiérrez

►

Orchids found in the area of
Machu Picchu
Photo: Courtesy Walter Wust

Orchids found in the area of Machu Picchu, some species of which remain unidentified
Photo: Courtesy Walter Wust

river banks. There are also high altitude palms of the genus *Geomoina* and arborescent ferns (*Cyarthea sp.*), as well as many orchids (nearly a hundred species) of the Cynthea genus, which flower throughout the year on both open ground and within the forest. Among the most beautiful orchids are *Masdevallia barlaeana* and *Maxillaria floribunda*. Among the bromeliads found in the sanctuary are *Puya weberbauerei sp.* and *Tillandsia rubra*, to name just two (Christensen 2002).

The Sanctuary's fauna varies depending on its life zone, of which there are ten. Among the birds there is of course the condor (*Vultur gryphus*), and more than sixteen species of hummingbird. Mammals include the "tanca taruca" deer (*Mazama chunyii*) and the puma (*Felis concolor*), the "tigrillo" (*Felis par-*

dalis) and species of monkey from the genuses *Cebus sp.*, *Saimiri sp.* and *Aotus* genus (the *Aotus* are in danger of extinction). Among the ophidians are the boa (Boa constrictor) and vipers from the *Bothrops* genus.

Several of the Sanctuary's fauna are in danger of extinction, including the cock-of-the-rock or "tunqui" (*Rupicola peruviana*), the spectacled bear (*Tremarctos ornatus*) and the otter (*Lutra longicaudis*), as well as the wild cat (*Felis colocolo*). (Source: INRENA / SINANPE, 1996).

To counteract the devastating impact on Machu Picchu represented by the enormous and growing influx of tourists to the site, as well as to protect the varied fauna and flora in the diverse life zones within the Machu Picchu Historical Sanctuary, some of which are threatened with extinction, the Na-

tional Institute of Culture (INC) and the National Institute for Natural Resources (INRENA) have elaborated a Master Plan for 2004-2005. This plan boasts a team of recognized experts in a number of fields. In this solid document, the sacred character of the space occupied by Machu Picchu is stressed, a theme highlighted by Johan Reinhard (1991, 2002) in a lucid and emphatic manner. It is important to underline that the document mentioned relies on the argument presented by Margaret Mould de Pease, emphasized in the Master Plan proposed by the INC-Cusco in December 2002, in that it covers the protection of the entire Machu Picchu Historical Sanctuary in place of the traditional focus which has been on the Machu Picchu ruins themselves as a tourist attraction of exceptional profitability.

When Hiram Bingham brought Machu Picchu to the world's attention in 1911, the land on which the ruins stand was privately owned. It belonged to Ignacio Ferro and his wife, who had acquired it from the Nadal family, who had registered the land as theirs when the Public Registry Office was first created.

But the history of the ownership of the site goes back centuries. In 1657 the Augustinian order took advantage of the fertile soils of Machu Picchu. Years later the area, known as

Silque, from Pomatales to Aobamba, belonged to the Spaniard Juan de Centeno, who donated it to the Bethlehemite Order, which owned the area until at least the second half of the 20th century. To this day, Julio Carlos Zavaleta bases his own claim to Machu Picchu and other nearby ruins on documentary evidence. When the Machu Picchu Historical Sanctuary was created in 1981, with its 32,592 hectares, these lands became the property of the state.

The Residence of the Inca, in Vitcos, during a festival that evokes its past
Photo: Federico Kauffmann Doig

Machu Picchu
and the "Incas of Vilcabamba"

Machu Picchu is situated in the region known as Vilcabamba, which in general terms extends northeast of Cuzco between the Apurímac and Urubamba rivers. The territory is bordered by the Vilcabamba Range which, like the topography of the Amazonian Andes in general, is characterised by steep slopes covered in lush tropical cloud forest vegetation. These green slopes contrast strikingly with the region's white peaks, such as Salcantay (6271 metres).

This region became the centre of neo-Inca resistance to the Spanish occupation of the Inca state. The campaign was fought between 1536 and 1572 by Manco Inca and his descendants: Sayri Tupac, Titu Cusi Yupanqui and Tupac Amaru (the First). This dynasty of neo-Inca sovereigns is referred to as the "Incas of Vilcabamba". As the historian Edmundo Guillén emphasises, Manco Inca's initial objective was the extermination of the Spanish and the recovery of the Inca state.

The military operations of the Incas of Vilcabamba were focused in the river basin of the same name, also known as Vitcos or Uiticus. With time the Pampaconas area also gained prominence. The key areas, in terms of the events that would take place in these river basins, were Rosaspata, where the archaeological sites of Vitcos and Ñustaispana (Niustaispana) are located, and Espiritupampa, where the majority of scholars believe the city of Vilcabamba the Old was founded

Manco Inca
meeting with
Pizarro when
the Spaniard
neared Cuzco
in 1533
**Drawing by
Guaman Poma
c.1600**

(c.1611), as well as Titu Cusi Yupanqui, with his celebrated *Ynstrucción* (1570) [*].

There are many more recent studies (Bingham 1948, pp.117-171, 1949, 2002, pp.93-144; Guillén 1974, 1977, 1978, 1981, 1984, 1994; Hemming 1970; Kubler 1947; Lee 2000; Mackehenie 1908-1913; Martín Rubio 1988; Pardo 1972; Regalado de Hurtado 1997; Savoy 1964; Vega 1963, 1964, 1980, 2000).

The work of Víctor Angles (1972, pp.73-154 and 239-280), as well as recounting the events in Vilcabamba, also describes the principal archaeological sites where historical events took place. Edmundo Guillén (1977, 1994) trekked in the region on two occasions in the footsteps of Manco Inca and his successors, and identified several of the sites where combat described in the chronicles took place.

With the same motive, María del Carmen Martín Rubio and Santiago del Valle Chousa also ventured into the region, identifying in 1997 the historic site of Rangaya or Layangalla, in the highlands north of Vitcos. They also claim to have located, together with the Cuzco-born archaeologist Octavio Fernández, the old settlement of Pampaconas (Valle 2005). In his book, Bingham tells of how in 1911 he passed through the village, but he found no remains of Inca constructions. After having identified in the surrounded area a plaza, walls and the remains of buildings, María del Carmen and Santiago del

Valle reasoned that this, and not the present-day settlement of Pampaconas, was the historic site of the same name cited by the chroniclers; the place where Titu Cusi Yupanqui finished dictating his celebrated "Ynstruccion" in 1570 and from where, two years later, the army of Hurtado de Arbieto launched its final attack on Vilcabamba the Old.

Santiago del Valle recounts how, continuing his explorations in 1998, he

by Manco Inca. Machu Picchu, beyond the geographical region of Vilcabamba, was not involved directly in the main events of the resistance, perhaps because it did not offer the enormous natural obstacles to access presented by the Vilcabamba and Pampacona river basins. Nevertheless, the depopulation of Machu Picchu may have been due to Manco Inca's recruitment campaign, or even those of his successors, as occurred in the Amaybamba valley.

An enormous amount of information regarding the Vilcabamba campaign has come down to us through the chronicles, often written by men who took part in the hostilities. Such is the case of Juan de Betanzos (1551-61/Part II, Chapters 28-34) who actually journeyed to Vilcabamba in 1558, Diego Rodríguez de Figueroa (1565) and Baltazar Ocampo Conejeros

(*) More information is supplied in the work of the mercenary Martín de Murúa (c.1600) and Phelipe Guaman Poma (c.1600). The former compiled, without a doubt, data from previous sources, including oral histories. Guaman Poma seems to have relied on oral history alone. Precise data, particularly with regard to the first teaching of the catechism and the location of the temple at Vilcabamba, were supplied by the Augustinian priest Antonio de la Calancha (1638). Although he wrote after the event, Calancha had access to early documents. Calancha did not have access to Murúa's writings, however, and therefore does not cite some of the events described in that chronicle. According to Calancha, the documents he used to describe the events in Vilcabamba were sent to the Vatican. There is no doubt that the detailed description of the execution in Cuzco of Tupac Amaru by Diego Francisco Altamirano (c.1700) is based on eyewitness accounts, except perhaps the speech purportedly made by Tupac Amaru before he was beheaded, with which the author seems to have embellished his tale. The work of Diego de Esquivel y Navia (c.1750) – the authentic Peruvian historian of the 18th century – although written long after the events described, is based on early documents. (The virtue of Calancha's work in particular is its chronological ordering of events). Esquivel y Navia has the virtue of having ordered for the first time the events of Vilcabamba in chronological order.

(1) Manco Inca's troops fighting at Cuzco. In the background Sacsahuaman, drawn as a walled tower **(Engraving by DeBry 1594)**. (2) Sacsahuaman and its terraces of enormous blocks **(Photo HB/Bildatlas)**. (3) The apostle Saint James collaborated with the Christians. (4) On that occasion, the Virgin Mary came down from heaven to the chamber where the Spanish had taken refuge in Cuzco
Coloured carving / Cuzco. Federico Kauffmann Doig archive

▲(1) ▼(2)

▼(3)

▼(4)

travelled through the territory west of present-day Pampaconas, an area never previously described (Valle 2005). The Pampaconas River flows into the Apurímac. Santiago del Valle explored Patibamba and Pintobamba, valleys to the north of the area's principal Apu, Mount Choquezafra (5,164 metres), and claims to have discovered the true location of Vilcabamba the Old (or Vilcabamba the Great). According to del Valle, the city was not situated in the area of Espíritupampa, as current consensus would have it.

Santiago del Valle also claims to have identified Wayna Pucara, the last fortress that protected the Inca capital of Vilcabamba, as well as the ruins of Marcanay, where the Spanish army rested on the day before the capture of the Inca's final refuge. Together with the archaeologist Wilbert Bolivar, and funded by Discovery Channel, in 2002 Santiago del Valle excavated for the first time the remains of an Inca religious building in the area. His explorations in Patibamba, aimed at identifying the complex

of structures and urban nucleus of what might turn out to be Vilcabamba the Old, would prove that the last refuge of the "Incas of Vilcabamba" was indeed located here and not at Espíritupampa.

Vincent R. Lee (1985, 1989, 2000) is the author of a very valuable work, which includes practically all the archaeological remains in the Vilcabamba and Pampaconas-Concebidayoc river basins. Roberto Samanez (Samanez and Zapata 1996) has produced immaculate plans of Ñustaispana or Yuracrumi (Iurakrumi), the principal shrine of the Incas of Vilcabamba.

The story of the neo-Incas of Vilcabamba really begins at the end of 1533, when Francisco Pizarro journeyed from Cajamarca to take control of Cuzco, the Inca capital (Varón 1996). Manco Inca went to meet Pizarro before he reached the city, in order to secure his succession to the throne as the legitimate successor of his father, the expansionist ruler Huayna Capac. Manco was also brother to Atahualpa and Huascar, who had been engaged in civil war when the Spanish arrived and were both now dead (Temple 1937-48). Pizarro decided to "crown" Manco Inca, knowing that a puppet Inca under his control could only be to his advantage. In Cuzco, Francisco Pizarro's two brothers, Gonzalo and Juan, demanded more and more gold from Manco. Gonzalo even insisted that the Inca give him his wife. In 1535, Manco Inca was accused of

conspiring against the Spanish and imprisoned.

Some months later, in 1536, Hernando Pizarro arrived in Cuzco and freed Manco Inca, with the condition that he remain in the city. However, Manco tricked Hernando, promising to bring him a gold corncob of predigious size from Yucay, and the latter allowed him to leave the city. In Yucay, Manco decided not to return to the city where he had suffered such humiliation and vowed to fight the Spanish. In Yucay and then in Calca, he convened the nobility and a mass of followers, who pledged themselves to his cause. It was in Calca that Manco Inca and his captains vowed to fight "to the death to throw the Spanish out of Peru" (Guillén 1984, p.291).

When he realized that Manco Inca had deceived him, Hernando Pizarro sent his brother Juan in pursuit at the head of a squadron of cavalry. In a daring manoeuvre, Pizarro crossed the river at Yucay. The neo-Inca troops on the other bank were forced to retreat, before regrouping and attacking the Spanish in force. After several skirmishes the Spanish withdrew, and their rearguard was harried all the way to Cuzco.

Encouraged by his victory, Manco Inca ordered his army to attack Cuzco, take the city and annihilate the Spanish force of 200 men. At the beginning of 1536, under the command of Villa Omo, Manco's troops occupied Sacsahuaman, and the great temple above the city became a fortress. The siege of Cuzco lasted for months. Meanwhile, troops loyal to Manco Inca unsuccessfully attacked the Spanish city of Lima.

In the fighting to expel the neo-Incas from Sacsahuaman Juan Pizarro was mortally wounded and died a few days later. As the Spanish gained the upper hand, one of the Inca captains, traditionally known as Cahuide, decided to kill himself rather than surrender. He wrapped himself in his cloak (*llacolla* = liacolia) and threw himself from the top of one of the towers of the fortress. The neo-Inca troops occupying Sacsahuaman were finally forced to withdraw. There are references in the chronicles of the 16th century that indicate Inca troops withdrew voluntarily because they had to return to their fields for the planting season. An anonymous author (Anonymous, 1539) has given us a firsthand account of the siege of Cuzco, as did Juan de Betanzos (1551-56).

The Spanish themselves were astonished that they had been able to save themselves, for they numbered just 200. Their incomprehension in the face of triumph gave rise to a myth. It was said that while the straw roofs of the city burned from the besiegers' arrows the Virgin Mary had come down from heaven to the Sunturwasi, where the Spanish had taken refuge. To save the trapped Spaniards, the Virgin had blinded the neo-Incas with ashes and extinguished the flames. It was said that the apostle Saint James had also appeared, gal-

On occasion the Spanish were forced to retreat
Drawing by Guaman Poma c.1600 / Not referring to the battle at Tambo specifically

Allegorical drawing representing the battles at Tambo, or Ollantaytambo
Ilustration from 19th century

The central sector of Ollantaytambo
Photo: Mylene d'Auriol

loping across the sky on his white horse and brandishing his sword at Manco Inca's warriors.

With the siege broken, Manco Inca retired with part of his force to Ollantaytambo, while the rest of his army returned to their fields. Hernando Pizarro, together with his brother Gonzalo, marched against Manco Inca. Their attack on Ollantaytambo failed, and during the fighting Manco Inca himself could be seen on horseback with a sword in his hand, exhorting his men.

Rodrigo Orgóñez in an engraving from Antonio de Herrera's 16th century chronicle
Drawing taken from Juan José Vega

(1) The Inca's Residence, in Vitcos
Photo: Federico Kauffmann Doig

(2) The Vilcabamba region
Federico Kauffmann Doig / Oscar Sakay

(1)

(2)

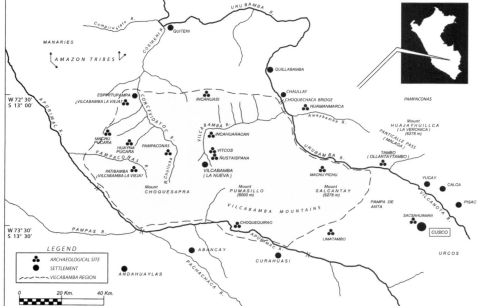

VILCABAMBA REGION

Rodrigo Orgóñez managed to defeat Manco Inca at Amaybamba, and the latter determined to retreat to a less easily accessible region. He crossed the Urubamba river via the Choquechaca o Chuquichaca (Tshuqitshaka) bridge near what is today the village of Chaullay, and advanced as far as Vitcos (or Uiticus), which was also the name once given to the Vilcabamba river. The prolonged neo-Inca resistance in the Vilcabamba mountains had begun, and it would not end until 1572.

In Vitcos, Manco Inca settled in the so-called Palace of the Inca, situated, according to the chronicles, at Choquepalta or Choquepalpa (Choquepata?), which the author prefers to call the Residence of the Inca, barely two kilometres from the shrine at Vitcos dedicated to the God of Water. Of the temple only part of the foundations remain, but the spectacular carved white rock (Yuracrumi or Ñustaispana) can still be seen. The shrine of the water god stands alongside extensive agricultural terracing, and it belongs to the Agricultural Sector of Vitcos. This complex is close to the village of Huancacalle and was occupied by Manco Inca, but not built by him. It was built during the time of the Inca state, in common with other administrative, ritual and production centres in the Vilcabamba region.

It was in Vitcos that Manco Inca was ambushed by Rodrigo Orgóñez during a ritual celebration. Manco Inca managed to escape by crossing the Pampaconas pass. In search of a

In April 1537, Diego de Almagro returned to Cuzco, while Francisco Pizarro remained absent. Almagro was returning from Chile, whence he had travelled in search of riches like those the conquistadors had found in Cuzco. He had launched his expedition in response to the Royal Warrant of 1534, which decreed that the territory conquered be divided between Almagro and Pizarro. The order divided the Inca state into New Castille and New Toledo, with New Castille going to Francisco

Pizarro and New Toledo to Diego de Almagro. The dividing line, however, was imprecise, and the two men disputed the possession of Cuzco. After his unsuccessful Chilean expedition, Almagro took control of Cuzco and imprisoned Hernando and Gonzalo Pizarro.

Three months after taking control of Cuzco, Almagro sent Rodrigo Orgóñez –or Orgoños, according to Juan José Vega (2000)– against Manco Inca, who retired from Ollantaytambo to Amaybamba.

The Shrine of the Water God, or Ñustaispana: (1 and 2) The great carved rock. (3) The paccha with its two channels. (4) The place where some substance flowed during the worship of water; according to tradition, a princess would urinate during the ceremony
Photos: Federico Kauffmann Doig; plans by Roberto Samanez Argumedo and Julinho Zapata

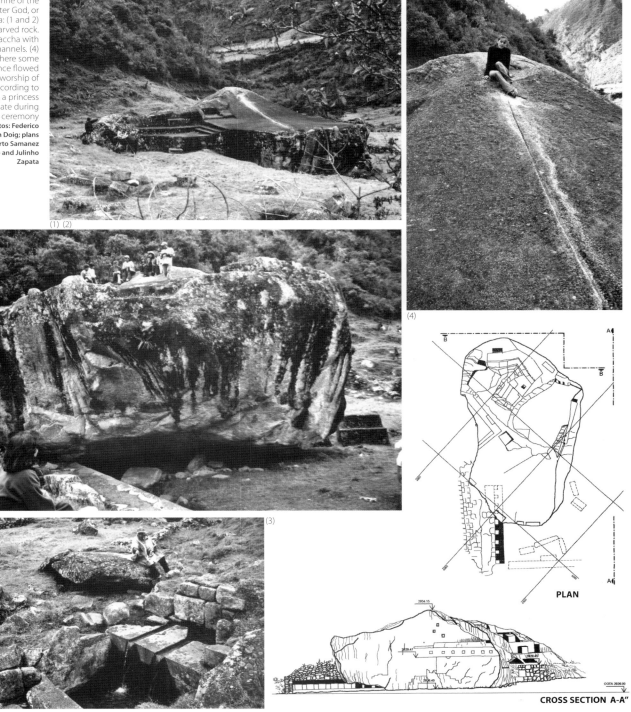

(1) (2)

(3)

(4)

PLAN

CROSS SECTION A-A"

Manco Inca retired after the battle at Tambo to the Vilcabamba region. He passed through Huamanmarca and crossed the Urubamba via the old bridge at Choquechaca
Photo of suspension bridge by Loren McIntry / L. and T. Engl

Huamanmarca
Photo: Federico Kauffmann Doig

somewhere nearby, that he built the neo-Inca city known as Vilcabamba. If the city was indeed sited at Espiritupampa, it would have been built in the foothills of the Amazonian Andes, some 1400 metres above sea level. Although the environment was alien to the highland dwelling neo-Incas, accustomed as they were to living at more than 3000 metres above sea level, the remote tropical forest eventually proved a wise choice.

The city founded by Manco Inca was known to the Spanish chroniclers as "Vilcabamba the Old". This epithet distinguishes the city from the town of the same name founded in 1572 by the Spanish at the headwaters of the Vilcabamba or Vitcos river after the defeat of the Vilcabamba Incas. Its full name was San Francisco de la Victoria de Vilcabamba, although

place even more remote and inaccessible than Vitcos, he may have headed for the area now known as Espiritupampa, unless he made for Patibamba (Valle 2005). It was here, or

it is more commonly known as Vilcabamba.

Vilcabamba the Old was avidly sought by scholars and explorers. Antonio Raimondi thought it might have been Choquequirao, but his hypothesis has since been dismissed. Hiram Bingham (1914, 1949) received information placing Vilcabamba the Old in the area known as Espiritupampa-Concebidayoc. He writes: "Don Pedro Duque (...) two of his informants indicated that a place called Concebidayoc (Espiritupampa) was a possible location for Vilcabamba the Old. Don Pedro told us that in 1902 López Torres, who had travelled extensively in the mountains in search of rubber, said he had discovered the ruins of an Inca city (in Espiritupampa-Concebidayoc)". But on visiting the site, Bingham did not realize the full extent of the ruins, hidden as they were

Plan: courtesy Vincent Lee

View of the central sector of the city of Vilcabamba the Old, which a virtual consensus of opinion identifies as the city founded by Manco Inca at Espiritupampa in the Amazonian Andes, adjacent to the Amazon basin, where ethnic groups distinct from the people of the Andes live.

The photos show a young Amazonian woman, a monkey hunted for food and a forest-dweller posing in front of the ruins of Vilcabamba the Old when Bingham visited the site

under thick vegetation, and in 1915 he decided that this could not be the location of Vilcabamba the Old. Later, Gene Savoy (1964, 1970) was guided to Espiritupampa by Cusco-born Antonio Santander, who was convinced that the ruins were those of Vilcabamba the Old. Santander estimated that the site covered an area of some 30 or 40 km2. Bingham, like Savoy, identified roof tiles at Espiritupampa. Because tiles had been introduced by the Spanish, Bingham reasoned that the city had been built by the Incas after the European invasion of Peru.

Later exploration from 1998 to 2005 by Santiago del Valle Chousa (2005), to the west of the present-day village of Pampaconas, has led to the claim that Vilcabamba the Old was not sited at Espiritupampa, but rather in the area of Patibamba, on the northern slopes of Mount Choquezafra (5,164 metres), which is the principal Apu of the region and dominates the nearby Pampaconas river basin, a tributary of the Apurímac, forty kilometres to the southeast of Espiritupampa.

Hernando Pizarro was freed by Diego de Almagro, but soon turned on his erstwhile captor. The ensuing civil war ended with the Battle of Las Salinas in April 1538 and the defeat of the Almagrists. Meanwhile, Francisco Pizarro had sent a Spanish force to Cuzco, reinforced by native auxiliaries, in the hope that his brothers would be able to capture or kill Manco Inca. Francisco Pizarro himself arrived in Cuzco shortly after the battle at Las Salinas.

The Spanish made repeated incursions into the Vilcabamba region in their attempts to annihilate the neo-Inca resistance
19th century illustration

The force sent by Pizarro in pursuit of Manco Inca was annihilated at the Battle of Orongoy in December 1538. After this victory, Manco Inca continued the struggle from several parts of the Vilcabamba region, and there are references, although they are vague, to sorties by the neo-Inca leader beyond his Vilcabamba stronghold. His mission was to skirmish with the Spanish, ambushing their caravans on the road between Cuzco and Lima, particularly along the left bank of the Apurímac river, between Cuzco and San Juan de la Frontera de Guamanga (Ayacucho). Although it is located on the very edge of the Vilcabamba region, in order to make their attacks on the Spanish, Manco Inca's troops must have occupied the ruins known today as Choquequirao. This site was mentioned by Cosme Bueno (c.1786) and Pablo José Oricain (1790), but the first description of the ruins was made by Eugenio de Lavandais (1834). In 1909 the city was explored by Hiram Bingham (1910), who dismissed Antonio Raimondi's theory (1874-1913) that the site was that of Vilcabamba the Old. In 1986, Roberto Samanez made excavations at Choquequirao, producing a detailed plan of the ruins which served as the basis for the restoration work carried out in 1998 and continued intensively in subsequent years under the auspices of Eliane Karp de Toledo and with the support of the Peru-France Debt Exchange Fund (Karp de Toledo 2004a; Lumbreras and Wust 2002). This vast complex stands above the right bank of the Apurímac, surrounded by mountains. Manco Inca must surely have occupied it, and the majority of the architecture at Choquequirao dates from the Inca period.

In order to control the neo-Inca ambushes, especially around Limatambo, Curahuasi, Abancay and Andahuaylas, Francisco Pizarro sent his brother Gonzalo to Vilcabamba, the focus of hostilities against Manco Inca. In the many skirmishes that followed, the Spanish emerged victorious. But the neo-Incas reorganized and counter-attacked again and again. One of the skirmishes may have taken place at Incahuaracana (Inkawarakana), near Puquiura, or perhaps at the Residence of the Inca in Vitcos. Although Gonzalo's troops won, they were unable to capture Manco Inca. However, Cura Ocllo, Manco Inca's first wife, together with other members of his family, was taken prisoner. After again failing to capture Manco Inca, Gonzalo returned to Cuzco with his prisoners. According to witnesses, including Pedro Pizarro, to protect herself against her captor's advances, Cura Ocllo smeared her body with faeces. On the road to Cuzco, she was condemned to death. Regarding the suffering of Cura Ocllo, Pedro Pizarro (1571) has this to say: "Marquéz was commanded to kill this woman of Manco Inca, and she was tied to a post and some Cañaris shot her with arrows until she died (…). The Spanish who were there said that this Indian never said a word as she died from the arrows shot at her".

The neo-Inca assaults on the roads between Cuzco and Ayacucho went on unabated after Gonzalo Pizarro retired from the Vilcabamba region. In fact, action was intensified and continued until 1539. Through this strategy, Manco Inca's followers were able to skirmish with the Spanish and at the same time provide themselves with supplies, even taking captured cattle and sheep into the Vilcabamba region. So it is not surprising to find that the neo-Incas were breeding European cattle and sheep as early as the mid-16th century, as confirmed by the chronicler Baltazar Ocampo Conejeros (c.1611), one of the eyewitnesses to the events in Vilcabamba.

In 1545, Manco Inca was assassinated by Diego Méndez, a Spaniard who, some years earlier, together with other defeated Almagrists after the Battle of Las Salinas in 1538, had sought refuge with the neo-Incas of Vilcabamba. Enraged by the death of their leader, the neo-Incas pursued the escaping Spaniards, capturing and beheading them all. Manco Inca, who took several days to die, lived to see the head of his assassin. The skulls of the executed Spaniards were still displayed at Vitcos as late as 1565, according to Diego Rodrí-

Cura Ocllo, the wife of Manco Inca, was captured and killed by the Spanish. Her clothing would have been similar to that of the woman in this illustration **Martín de Murúa. MS Duke of Wellington (c.1600) / Courtesy of Juan Ossio**

Choquequirao, from where the Incas of Vilcabamba launched guerrilla operations

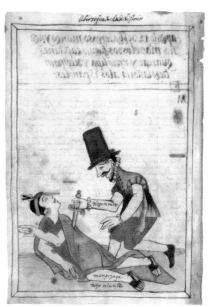

In 1544 Manco Inca was killed by Diego Méndez, an Almagrist who had been accepted at Manco's court after the defeat of Almagro at the battle of Chupas (1542)
Illustration by Martín de Murúa (c.1600) / Galvin Collection. Courtesy of Juan Ossio

Yucay, restored by Arminda Gibaja. Three years after installing himself in Yucay, Sayri Tupac died from suspected poisoning.

After Sayri Tupac had yielded to the Spanish crown his brother, Titu Cusi Yupanqui, assumed the government of Vilcabamba. He showed himself to be warlike, and attacks against Spanish travellers between Cuzco and Ayacucho intensified. In response to the insistence of the Spanish crown, the Viceroy Diego López de Zúñiga, the Count of Nieva, sent ambassadors with gifts to negotiate with Titu Cusi Yupanqui.

With López de Zúñiga's death in 1564, Lope García de Castro became viceroy, and was to govern until 1569. The new viceroy considered the neo-Incas of Vilcabamba responsible for attacks on the Chiriguanos and Charcas, as well as against the natives of Chile, and added charges of conspiracy against the chieftains of Jauja.

In April of 1565, Titu Cusi Yupanqui allowed Diego Rodríguez Figueroa, who was acting under the orders of Juan de Matienzo, to enter the Vilcabamba region for a meeting. A few weeks after this interview, Matienzo himself met with Titu Cusi Yupanqui at the Chuquichaca bridge. But the meeting did not achieve Matienzo's objective of pacifying Vilcabamba (Lohmann 1941; Regalado de Hurtado 1997). Nevertheless, during the mandate of Lope García de Castro, in 1568, Titu Cusi Yupanqui allowed priests to enter the region under his control. He allowed himself to be baptised in a ceremony held at Puquiura (Regalado 1997) or, according to

guez de Figueroa (1565), who saw them on his way to negotiate with Titu Cusi Yupanqui on the orders of Juan de Matienzo.

Manco Inca was succeeded by his son Sayri Tupac, who continued the guerrilla campaign against the Spanish until, in 1558, he agreed to leave Vilcabamba. He went to Cuzco and from there to Lima, where he was granted an audience with the Viceroy Andrés Hurtado de Mendoza. Returning to Cuzco, he was given a large estate in the fertile Yucay valley as a reward for having abandoned Vilcabamba. He was also granted other privileges. For example, and despite having been baptised, he was allowed to marry his sister Cusi Huarcay, thereby continuing the tradition of incest institutionalised by the ruling dynasty of the Inca state. The remains of Sayri Tupac's palace can still be seen in

Sayri Tupac met with Viceroy Andrés Hurtado de Mendoza in Lima (1558) and agreed to leave Vilcabamba. One of the conditions was the Spanish acceptance of his marriage to his sister Cusi Huarcay, a dynastic incest practiced by his ancestors
Drawing by Guaman Poma c.1600

While some descendants of the Inca nobility collaborated with the Spanish, Manco Inca and his descendants at Vilcabamba continued to resist **(Oil painting from Santa Ana church in Cuzco)**.

The Incas also faced ethnic Amazonians in the lowland forests, who they also recruited to their ranks Scene from a quero or wooden vase of indigenous manufacture, from the 16th or 17th century / **Museo Nacional de Arqueología, Antropología e Historia del Perú / Drawing by Pablo Carrera**

Estrudicion a señor
da, serla S. de Caima, una
delas preciosas Joyas con q̃
el Emperador Carlos V en tri
gurciò este Ymperia Y que al pa
sar por este Sitio, hablò por
dos ocasiones alos Yndios
que la conducian: Caim
Caim, i no la pudie
ron mouer mas

es el Año D. Jacinto Carbajal, Por mandado d̃ l
po de Zamacola y Jaureoui Cura de Caima. Año de 1780.

Tito Cusi Yupanqui, Manco Inca's successor, allowed missionaries to enter the Vilcabamba region, and was even baptised himself
Scene taken from an oil painting in the church at Cayma, in Arequipa
Photo: Courtesy of Banco de Crédito del Perú

Upon the death of Titu Cusi, The friar Diego Ortiz was tortured for not having been able to resuscitate him. The Augustinian chronicler Antonio de la Calancha (1638) speaks at length of the martyrdom of Ortiz
Illustration / Antonio de la Calancha (1638)

CORONICA
MORALIZADA
DEL ORDEN DE
SAN AVGVSTIN EN EL
PERV, CON SVCESOS
EGENPLARES EN ESTA
MONARQVIA.
DEDICADA A NVESTRA SEÑORA
de Gracie, fingular Patrona i Abogada de la dicha Orden.

COMPVESTA POR EL MVY REVERENDO
Padre Maestro Fray Antonio de la Calancha de la misma Orden, i Defasidor actual.

DIVIDESE ESTE PRIMER TOMO EN QVATRO
libros; lleva tablas de Capitulos, i lugares de la fagrada Escritura.

Año   1638.

CON LICENCIA

En Barcelona: Por Pedro LACAVALLERIA, en la calle de la Librería.

Edmundo Guillén (1994), in Ragalla or Layangalla, between Lucma and Pampaconas, which may correspond to the modern village of Huancacalle. At his baptism, Titu Cusi Yupanqui received the name Diego de Castro. Scholars suspect Titu Cusi Yupanqui of only wishing to appear Christian (Regalado 1997). Shortly afterwards, still in 1568, the friar Marcos García was sent to instruct Titu Cusi in the Christian faith.

A year later, in 1569, the Augustinian friar Diego de Ortiz entered Vilcabamba to assist Marcos García. Soon afterwards, in Pampaconas in 1570, Titu Cusi Yupanqui finished dictating his celebrated *Ynstrucción*, begun in 1568, which was published by Luis Millones in 1985 (Titu Cusi Yupanqui 1570) and analysed by Liliana Regalado (1981). In the writing and translation of his *Ynstrucción*, Titu Cusi Yupanqui was assisted by Marcos García and the *mestizo* Martín Pando, who acted as the Inca's secretary; according to Edmundo Guillén (1994), these events took place in San Salvador de Vilcabamba. Titu Cusi Yupanqui took a dislike to the friar Marcos García, who insisted that he adopt Christian ways and stop worshipping his traditional idols, as well as abandon other customs abominable to the Church. This grudge must have been exacerbated still further when Marcos García proceeded to exorcize and burn Ñustaispana, the most important shrine in the Vilcabamba region, an act which he repeated in the company of the friar Diego de Ortiz

(Calancha 1638). This shrine, as we have already mentioned, is located in Vitcos, at Rosaspata / Chuquipalta (Chuquipata or Chuquipanpa?), near Puquiura.

Such behaviour must have irritated Titu Cusi Yupanqui, which would explain his decision to expel Marcos García from Vilcabamba.

Sometime in mid-1571, Titu Cusi Yupanqui died at Puquiura from an unspecified disease. The neo-Incas asked Friar Diego de Ortiz to bring him back to life, for he had said that his all-powerful god was capable of bringing back the dead. When he showed himself unable to resuscitate the deceased Inca, the friar was tortured to death. Diego Ortiz is venerated as Peru's first martyr.

On the death of Titu Cusi Yupanqui in 1571, the government of Vilcabamba fell to Tupac Amaru, another of Manco Inca's sons (known as Tupac Amaru I, to distinguish him from Tupac Amaru II, who two hundred years later unleashed a revolution against the abuses suffered by the indigenous people of Peru).

The Viceroy Francisco Toledo travelled to Cuzco from Lima in 1571, determined to end once and for all the existence of the "state" of Vilcabamba. After initial failure, he commissioned Tilano Anaya to go to Vilcabamba as an ambassador carrying letters to Tupac Amaru. The Inca refused to negotiate with Anaya, and the neo-Incas guarding the Choquechaca bridge, the "gateway" to Vilcabamba, killed the ambassador. Toledo's response was immediate: he declared war on Tupac Amaru. The viceroy commissioned Martín Hurtado de Arbieto to go into Vilcabamba at the head of a battalion of Spaniards and Cañari and Chachapoyan natives; ethnic groups whose alliance with the Spanish has been recorded by the historian Waldemar Espinosa (1967).

Martín Hurtado de Arbieto and his troops repaired the bridge at Chuquichaca and entered the Vilcabamba region, defeating the neo-Incas in combat at Cayaochaca, according to Edmundo Guillén (1994), based on an original document quoted by John Hemming (1970).

Anxious to kill or capture Tupac Amaru, the Spanish continued their advance. They occupied the area of Pampaconas, in the upper stretches of the river of the same name. Leaving

After his capture Tupac Amaru
was taken to Cuzco
Drawing by Guaman Poma c.1600

Tupac Amaru was tried in Cuzco on the
orders of Viceroy Toledo
Be it legend or truth, it is said that the Viceroy Toledo...
Drawing by Guaman Poma c.1600

...on his return to Spain, was berated by the monarch,
who had sent him to Peru to serve kings
and not to kill them
Drawing: Guaman Poma c.1600

Pampaconas and heading towards the Amazon forest, they advanced as far as the city of Vilcabamba the Old, passing first through the village of Marcanay, just 10 kilometres from their objective. They finally occupied the city founded by Manco Inca on July 14th 1572.

As the Spaniards approached, Tupac Amaru managed to escape yet again, together with his women and closest followers. Captain Martín de Loyola (Martín Oñaz García de Loyola), on the orders of Martín Hurtado de Arbieto, pursued Tupac Amaru relentlessly. He captured his quarry in the Amazon forest, moments before he was due to board a raft and disappeared into the Amazon basin. Shortly after the capture of Tupac Amaru, the Spanish, to commemorate their triumph, founded the city of San Francisco de la Victoria de Vilcabamba in the Vilcabamba or Vitcos valley. With the capture of Tupac Amaru, Vilcabamba the Old was abandoned. In 1572, in recognition of his efforts, Martín Hurtado de Arbieto was named "governor, captain general and justice" of the Vilcabamba region.

With Loyola carrying the *Punchao* idol confiscated from him, Tupac Amaru was conveyed to Cuzco. This scene is captured in a drawing by Guaman Poma (c.1600). Through the intervention of Toledo and by way of reward, Martín de Loyola was married to the wealthy and much coveted Beatriz Clara Coya, Tupac Amaru's niece and the only daughter of Sayri Tupac (Rostworowski 1970; Temple 1950).

Tupac Amaru was beheaded in Cuzco in September 1572, after being baptised and christened Felipe. With the death of this direct descendant of the Inca sovereigns, the Vilcabamba dynasty was extinguished forever, together with Manco Inca's dream of expelling the Spanish from Peru and restoring the Inca state.

The marriage of Martín de Loyola to Beatriz Clara Coya, the niece of Tupac Amaru, who Loyola had captured shortly before
Painting in the Jesuit Church of Cuzco
Photo: Ruperto Márquez

The Inca State and Machu Picchu:
Historical Context

As already explained, it is the author's contention that Machu Picchu was an important element in an Inca state project to expand their agricultural frontiers into areas of the Amazonian Andes, situated between 2000 and 3000 metres above sea level, and close to Cuzco along the course of the Vilcanota or Urubamba river.

Judging by its architectural style, together with the artifacts found there and documentary evidence, Machu Picchu can be placed in the Historic Inca period, between 1438 and 1532, when the Spanish arrived in Peru. The Inca state spread from its capital, Cuzco, in a process of rapid expansion during which the Incas conquered the many nations inhabiting the Andes mountains and the coastal belt, beyond the frontiers of modern Peru. All of these nations had been fighting among themselves since time immemorial, including the Incas.

The ancestors of the sovereigns of the Inca state were believed to have emerged from the womb of the Earth Goddess, or Pachamama, via caves symbolising her vagina and located in Tamputoco (Tampu T'oqo), according to the myths surrounding the origin of the Inca nation. From there they migrated as far as the Cuzco valley.

Like the other nations that inhabited the territory of the Inca state, the Incas were the heirs to an ancestral Peruvian civilization going back some 4000 years. The first cultures left behind architecture of monumental proportions like that found at Caral / Chupacigarro. This dawning civilization grew and by the first millennium before Christ it had developed into the Chavín / Cupisnique culture, the basis for the subsequent development of ancient Peruvian, or Andean, cultures. In the first half of the first millennium after Christ, the Paracas-Nazca and Moche cultures emerged on the coast, with their unrivalled achievements in weaving and pottery. At the same time, on the shores of Lake Titicaca, the Tiahuanaco culture developed, characterised by its architecture and its gigantic sculptures like the Sun Gate, which was carved from a single block of stone and decorated with magical-religious figures. By the second half of the first millennium after Christ, the Tiahuanaco culture had spread throughout southern Peru and northern Chile. It reached the site of present-day Ayacucho, where it expanded with new characteristics over a large area, occupying parts of the coast and the highlands in what is today central and southern Peru. This expansion-

ist culture emerging from Ayacucho is known as the Wari, or Tiahuanaco-Huari, if we are to remember its roots in Tiahuanaco. During the first centuries of the second millennium after Christ, the Tiahuanaco-Huari state, with its centre at Huari (Ayacucho), and the Tiahuanaco, based in the Titicaca basin, began to wane, with the re-emergence throughout their territories of ethnic identities that managed to emancipate themselves and restore their ancient traditions and forms of government. But, in their turn, these emancipated nations developed their own aspirations, hoping to enlarge their territories by conquering those of their neighbours. Eventually one of these nations, the Incas, would emerge triumphant and incorporate the others into a centrally governed Inca state.

This final phase of ancient Peruvian civilization was ruled by a dynasty of thirteen sovereigns, or Incas (Inykas) from Manco Capac (Manko Qhapaq), its mythical founder, to Atahualpa (Atawailpa), who was executed by the Spanish in 1533.

The expansion from Cuzco that formed the Inca state began in 1438 with the ruler Pachacutec, the ninth sovereign, or *Inca*, of the Inca dynasty. With him ends the phase known as

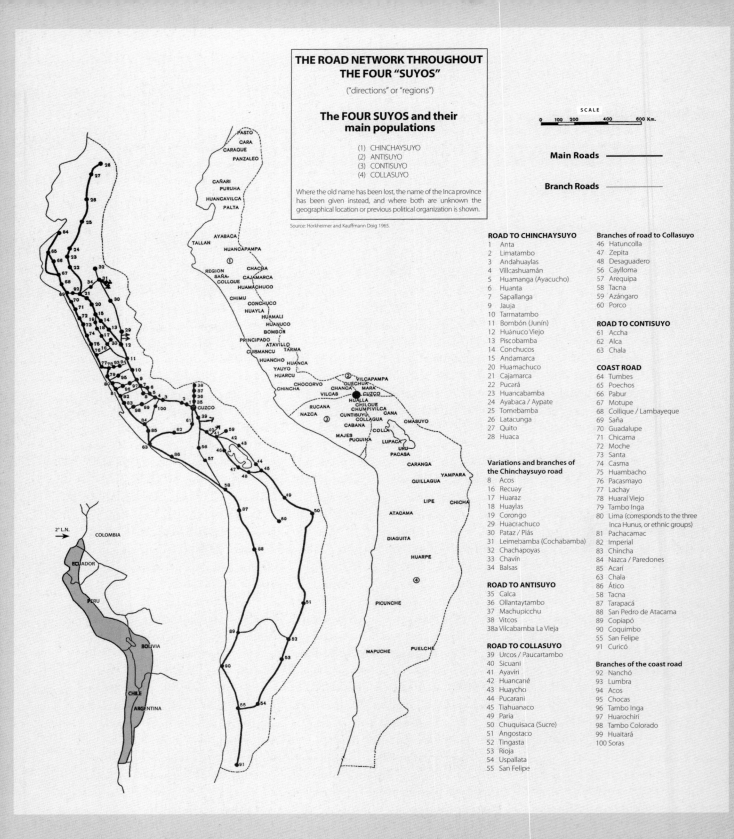

THE ROAD NETWORK THROUGHOUT THE FOUR "SUYOS"

("directions" or "regions")

The FOUR SUYOS and their main populations

(1) CHINCHAYSUYO
(2) ANTISUYO
(3) CONTISUYO
(4) COLLASUYO

Where the old name has been lost, the name of the Inca province has been given instead, and where both are unknown the geographical location or previous political organization is shown.

Source: Horkheimer and Kauffmann Doig 1965.

SCALE
0   100 200   400   600 Km.

Main Roads —————

Branch Roads —————

ROAD TO CHINCHAYSUYO
1   Anta
2   Limatambo
3   Andahuaylas
4   Villcashuamán
5   Huamanga (Ayacucho)
6   Huanta
7   Sapallanga
9   Jauja
10 Tarmatambo
11 Bombón (Junín)
12 Huánuco Viejo
13 Piscobamba
14 Conchucos
15 Andamarca
20 Huamachuco
21 Cajamarca
22 Pucará
23 Huancabamba
24 Ayabaca / Aypate
25 Tomebamba
26 Latacunga
27 Quito
28 Huaca

Variations and branches of the Chinchaysuyo road
8   Acos
16 Recuay
17 Huaraz
18 Huaylas
19 Corongo
29 Huacrachuco
30 Pataz / Piás
31 Leimebamba (Cochabamba)
32 Chachapoyas
33 Chavín
34 Balsas

ROAD TO ANTISUYO
35 Calca
36 Ollantaytambo
37 Machupicchu
38 Vitcos
38a Vilcabamba La Vieja

ROAD TO COLLASUYO
39 Urcos / Paucartambo
40 Sicuani
41 Ayaviri
42 Huancané
43 Huaycho
44 Pucarani
45 Tiahuanaco
49 Paria
50 Chuquisaca (Sucre)
51 Angostaco
52 Tingasta
53 Rioja
54 Uspallata
55 San Felipe

Branches of road to Collasuyo
46 Hatuncolla
47 Zepita
48 Desaguadero
56 Caylloma
57 Arequipa
58 Tacna
59 Azángaro
60 Porco

ROAD TO CONTISUYO
61 Accha
62 Alca
63 Chala

COAST ROAD
64 Tumbes
65 Poechos
66 Pabur
67 Motupe
68 Collique / Lambayeque
69 Saña
70 Guadalupe
71 Chicama
72 Moche
73 Santa
74 Casma
75 Huambacho
76 Pacasmayo
77 Lachay
78 Huaral Viejo
79 Tambo Inga
80 Lima (corresponds to the three Inca Hunus, or ethnic groups)
81 Pachacamac
82 Imperial
83 Chincha
84 Nazca / Paredones
85 Acarí
63 Chala
86 Ático
58 Tacna
87 Tarapacá
88 San Pedro de Atacama
89 Copiapó
90 Coquimbo
55 San Felipe
91 Curicó

Branches of the coast road
92 Nanchó
93 Lumbra
94 Acos
95 Chocas
96 Tambo Inga
97 Huarochirí
98 Tambo Colorado
99 Huaitará
100 Soras

The Inca dynasty comprised thirteen sovereigns and not fourteen, as represented by this painting

Triunfo Evangelico, nueva
exaltacion de la fee, glorias de la SS.ma Cruz,
consequidas en el dia sagrado de su invencion en este nu
ebo mundo el año de 1530. Por el N.P.Fr. Viçente de Valuerde
primer Obispo del Peru y uno de los siete Missioneros q̃ cõquis
taron este Reyno, embiados por el S.or Emperador Carlos.V. el qual

In Cajamarca the
priest Valverde
offered the bible
to Atahualpa,
moments before
Pizarro and his men
captured the Inca
**Oil painting attributed
to Diego Quispe Tito
Photo: Banco de
Crédito del Perú ("El
Barroco Peruano",
p. 216)**

▶

The Inca was
captured by
Pizarro's force
in November
1532
**Painting by Camilo
Blas**

▶

To free himself,
Atahualpa
offered to fill
a room once
with gold and
twice with
silver. Fearing
the reaction of
the natives, the
Spanish tried
him before the
ransom was
completed
(1533)
**Sketch from N.G.S.
/ Loren McIntry**

Inca Legendary, and the Inca Historic phase begins. Pachacutec enlarged the city of Cuzco, the administrative and religious capital of the Inca state founded by the mythical Manco Capac. Pachacutec and Tupac Inca Yupanqui (Thupaq Inyka Iupanki), who succeeded him, incorporated by diplomacy or force the nations that would comprise the Inca state, nations already linked by a common ancient cultural tradition.

Tupac Inca Yupanqui was succeeded by Huayna Capac, whose long political career lasted from 1493 until his death in 1525. The enormous extension of the Inca state under his predecessor sealed Huayna Capac's fate: he was destined to deal with continual uprisings by the nations under Inca rule. He fought hard to maintain the empire, punishing rebels ruthlessly. Uprisings in what is now Ecuador allowed Huayna Capac to establish the northern limit of his territory: he annexed the region of the Gulf of Guayaquil, northern Ecuador and the territory of the Chachapoyas. It is thought that his death was caused by smallpox, a disease that spread through the Americas like a plague after the arrival of the Spanish in the Caribbean. His mummified remains were transported from Quito to Cuzco.

Huayna Capac left behind hundreds of children, two of whom disputed the throne: Huascar and Atahualpa (1525-1532). When the ensuing fratricidal war seemed finally to be drawing to a close in Atahualpa's favour, the Spanish invaders, captained by Francisco Pizarro, captured the Inca at Cajamarca. Months later, in 1533, he was executed.

Atahuallpa's funeral. Some women voluntarily sacrificed themselves during the wake, following the Inca tradition called "necropompa" by Carlos Araníbar
Oil painting by Luis Montero: Museo de Arte, Lima

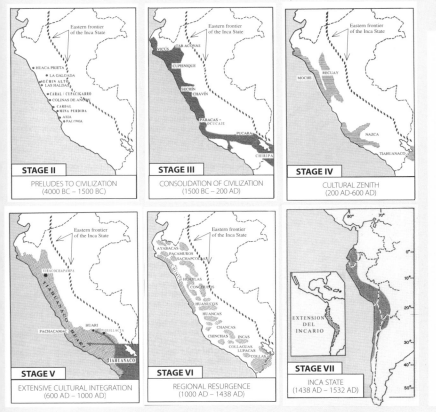

STAGE II	STAGE III	STAGE IV
PRELUDES TO CIVILIZATION (4000 BC – 1500 BC)	CONSOLIDATION OF CIVILIZATION (1500 BC – 200 AD)	CULTURAL ZENITH (200 AD-600 AD)
STAGE V	STAGE VI	STAGE VII
EXTENSIVE CULTURAL INTEGRATION (600 AD – 1000 AD)	REGIONAL RESURGENCE (1000 AD – 1438 AD)	INCA STATE (1438 AD – 1532 AD)

STAGE I: PRIMITIVE AGE (15000 BC – 4000 BC)
Synonyms: Stone Age / Hunter Stage / Pre-Agrarian Age / Archaic.
In this stage cultural knowledge was simple, restricted above all to the making of stone tools, which for thousands of years would be perfected to make them more efficient and decorative. The people who spread along the coast and into the highlands came originally from Asia, having migrated to the Americas across the Bering Strait. Their social structure was patriarchal. They left examples of cave paintings, which were believed to assist the hunt through magical means. The paintings depicted hunting scenes, which were drawn or painted on rock walls. Time was spent hunting for food, fishing and gathering vegetables. Important known sites: Lauricocha, Paiján, Toquepala…

In the Old World: Primitive culture in the Old World goes back to the dawn of humanity and in general terms was the same in Africa, Europe and Asia. The advance from the Paleolithic to the Neolithic period occurred some 10,000 years ago in Asia Minor. Neolithic man began to plant crops and domesticate animals, which in time gave way to the ancient civilizations.

STAGE IV: CULTURAL ZENITH (200 AD-600 AD)
Synonyms: Classical Epoch /Early Intermediate / Regional Flourishing.
This stage was characterised by its artistic and artisan splendour, particularly in the cultural expression of the Moche, Nazca and Classic Tiahuanaco (Titicaca). Both pottery and textiles served above all as magical-religious emblems, artistically interpreted. The geometrical crest of a wave symbol of the Water God was particularly widespread, as was the symbol of the Earth Goddess, expressed with a stepped design inspired by the agricultural terracing built in her honour. Sometimes both emblems were represented in a combined form, in a throne, or *ushnu*, upon which the Water God appeared standing, as in the case of the central figure of the Sun Gate at Tiahuanaco. On other occasions they appeared as a combined crest of a wave and step logo. Society was hierarchical. Increasingly efficient food production led to accelerated population growth, which in turn led to warfare between ethnic groups and domination.

In the Old World: Propagation of Christianity. Roman Empire / Barbarians.

STAGE V: EXTENSIVE CULTURAL INTEGRATION (600 AD – 1000 AD)
Synonyms: Middle Horizon / Tiahuanaco- Huari, Wari.
This stage was characterised by the formation of governments across a wide geographical area, especially in the case of Tiahuanaco-Huari and, to a lesser degree, Tiahuanaco Expansionist. Expansionism was inspired by the need to guarantee, through power, satisfactory food production for a growing population which consequently faced greater natural hardship: a poor territory for crops adversely affected by the El Niño phenomenon. Important centres: Huari, Piquillacta, Viracochapampa. The term Tiahuanaco-Huari, and not just Wari, derives from the fact that the expansionist phenomenon that had its power centre at Huari, near present-day Ayacucho, began at Tiahuanaco in Titicaca and spread to Ayacucho.

In the Old World: Byzantine culture, Mohammed (571 – 632 AD) and Islam. Establishment of feudalism in Europe.

CIVILIZATION IN TIME AND SPACE

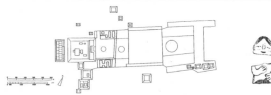

STAGE II: PRELUDES TO CIVILIZATION (4000 BC – 1500 BC)
Synonyms: Inferior Formative / Pre-Ceramic / Initial Period.
The beginning of food production, which previously had only been gathered. Incipient technology and the cultivation of just a few species of plants. In high Andean areas American members of the camel family are domesticated, and on the coast fishing becomes intensive. New food strategies meant more guaranteed nutrition, which brought population growth. Population grew in proportion to agricultural technological development and led to the appearance of the first forms of civilization. In ancient Peru, these cultures expressed themselves in the form of enormous architectural centres, built for administration and food production as well as the rituals and cults aimed at propitiating food production. Here the governing class lived, performing public ceremonies, and food surplus was stored. Sites on the central and northern coast: Caral / Chupacigarro, Cardal, Minaperdida etc. Pottery making was unknown (Pre-Ceramic Stage), as was metalwork, and textiles were simple. It was Rosa Fung who first deduced that the monumental architecture of this stage constituted the earliest basis for Peruvian civilization.

In the Old World: In Mesopotamia and Egypt, the beginning of pottery and metalwork around 5000 BC. The city of Ur (4300 BC). The Bronze Age (2900 BC). Pyramid of Cheops, 137 metres high (2580 BC). The wheel. Cuneiform writing. Written alphabet (2300 BC). Minoan civilization (2000 BC).

STAGE III CONSOLIDATION OF CIVILIZATION / or the "Wiraqotcha Movement" (1500 BC – 200 AD)
Synonyms: Early Horizon / Formative / Chavín.
In this stage all the cultural knowledge that characterises ancient Peruvian civilization is perfected and finally spread throughout the Central Andes, from the coast to the highlands. This great cultural movement was unleashed by ever growing population density which led to pressure to establish a socio-economic order that would guarantee food production. Its establishment was based on a number of magical-religious beliefs, expressed in the art of Chavín / Cupisnique and Chiripa, which flourished in the highlands of present-day Bolivia. To name this stage, we use the synonym *Wiraqotsha Movement*. This includes Andean Bolivia (Chiripa) and was the main driving force behind the subsequent development of Peruvian, or Andean, civilization, which until the arrival of the Spanish remained largely unchanged structurally, although it was subject to historical change due to the breaking time and again of unifying stages.

In the Old World: Assyrians, use of iron (1000 BC). Age of the Hebrew Prophets (800 BC). Confucius (551-479 BC). Greeks: Pericles, Socrates, Plato (300-500 BC).

STAGE VI: REGIONAL RESURGENCE (1000 AD – 1438 AD)
Synonym: Late Intermediate.
The unity of government of the previous stage fractured, giving way to the formation of states, such as Chimu and Chincha on the coast. In the highlands, the territorially extensive Yaro culture emerged in the central and northern highlands. Its wide diffusion can be detected in monumental architecture employing large square stones held in place by *pachillas* (wedge stones): Yayno, Marcahuamachuco, etc. Besides this ethnic group, throughout the highlands smaller nations such as the Huancas, Chocorbos, etc, were settled. Also during this phase, still limited to the Cuzco region, the Inca ethnic group developed, and would play a central role in the next stage of civilization. Despite warfare and rivalry, the socio-economic and religious legacy of the *Wiraqotsha Movement* continued on course.

In the Old World: The Holy Roman Germanic Empire. The Crusades. Gothic Art. Creation of universities (XII and XIII centuries).

STAGE VII: INCA STATE (1438 AD – 1532 AD)
Synonyms: Late Horizon / Tahuantinsuyo / Inca Empire.
In the context of the struggles of the previous stage, unleashed principally to solve the food problem caused by a growth in population, and causing ethnic groups to attempt to absorb their neighbours, the Incas, who originally occupied the Cuzco valley, emerged as the dominant force. The phenomenon of Inca expansion began in earnest with the sovereign Pachacutec in 1438, and culminated with the creation of the Inca state. This state eventually extended from southern Colombia as far as Maule in Chile – over 4000 kilometres. One hundred years later it was culturally and politically dismantled by the Spanish conquest. The socio-political and religious model of the *Wiraqotsha Movement* was continued under the Incas, perhaps because nature itself had not changed, and demographic growth was driven by advances in agricultural technology and, above all, because the established cultural model was an adequate one.

In the Old World: Printing 1440. Fall of the Byzantine Empire (1461). Luther (1483-1546). Discovery of the Americas (1492).

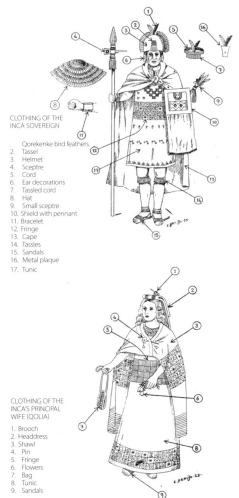

CLOTHING OF THE
INCA SOVEREIGN

1. Qorekenke bird feathers.
2. Tassel
3. Helmet
4. Sceptre
5. Cord
6. Ear decorations
7. Tassled cord
8. Hat
9. Small sceptre
10. Shield with pennant
11. Bracelet
12. Fringe
13. Cape
14. Tassles
15. Sandals
16. Metal plaque
17. Tunic

CLOTHING OF THE
INCA'S PRINCIPAL
WIFE (QOLIA)

1. Brooch
2. Headdress
3. Shawl
4. Pin
5. Fringe
6. Flowers
7. Bag
8. Tunic
9. Sandals

It is thought that Atahualpa, while a prisoner in Cajamarca and afraid that Huascar might ally himself with the Spanish, secretly ordered that he be killed on his way to Cuzco to meet the Spanish. These events marked the end of the Inca state, and opened the way to the westernization of Peru.

When the Spanish arrived, the Inca state was divided into four *suyos*, or quarters. Tahuantinsuyo (Tawantinsuio), or the country of the four regions, extending 4000 kilometres from north to south along the Pacific coast and the Andes mountains. That is, from southern Colombia to the north of Chile and north-western Argentina, including parts of highland Bolivia and Ecuador. From Cuzco, roads went to the four great regions of the state: Chinchaysuyo (Tshintshaisuio), Collasuyo (Qoiliasuio), Contisuyo (Kuntisuio) and Antisuyo (Antisuio). In total, the road network covered some 23,000 kilometres.

State works were carried out under the *mita* system (*mitmaq*), an obligatory labour tax organised on a rotor basis. The general population was also subject to another form of taxation, consisting of the handing over to the state of two thirds of the harvest from every family smallholding. This produce went to the nobility and the priesthood, and the surplus was stored for distribution in years of food shortage, which occurred often due to the El Niño phenomenon, which affects this part of the world drastically.

The administration of taxes and of the state in general was recorded on *quipus (khipu)*, a unique system of knotted cords.

In order to better organise the payment of tribute, the population was grouped into units of five, ten, one hundred, a thousand and ten thousand individuals. At the head of these groups was a state official. Labour was also divided according to age. Labour was obligatory and to work was seen as a virtue.

There was no money and all precious metals belonged to the state and were used to make emblematic figures for use in worship and to decorate the elite. Only very special services were rewarded with precious metals. Sumptuous weavings and even women were also given as gifts. There was no concept of inheritance, and each generation had to build their own home and clothe themselves. Each sovereign was buried with all his belongings, including his wives and closest servants (Araníbar 1970). This custom can be traced back some three thousand years; without it the treasures of Sipán would never have existed.

In common with their predecessors, from whom they inherited their knowledge, the Incas were pre-eminent farmers. They built terracing to convert arid slopes into fertile fields. On the coast, the valleys were irrigated on what was often an enormous scale, such as the La Cumbre canal, which was 105 kilometres long. The Incas also inherited the knowledge required to grow an infinity of plants, such as maize (*Zea mayz*), potatoes (*Solanum tuberosum*) and other tubers. They also herded llamas (*Lama glana*) and alpacas (*Lama pacos*), members of the camel family first domesticated 7000 years ago and still used for transport, food and wool.

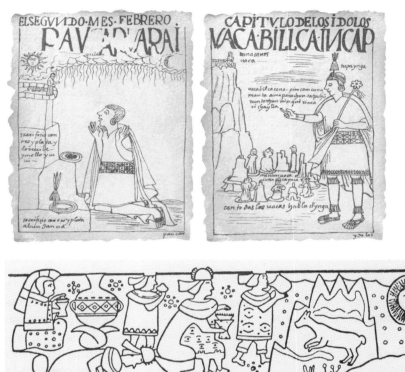

◄
Two drawings by Guaman Poma (c.1600) showing the worship of the entity belived to have controlled atmospheric conditions.
One of the drawings showing the sovereign in the company of lower order divine beings is eloquent in this respect, for it attempts to discover which of them was responsible for unleashing atmospheric catastrophes.

▼
The Water God personified by the Sun. The sun, among clouds, presides over the ceremony in his honour. He makes it rain and the drops nourish the river, from which irrigation canals run to the crops
Quero of indigenous manufacture (16th century?)

▼
Emblem of the Water God in the form of the crest of a wave, linked to the emblem of the Earth Goddess or Pachamama, which is inspired by the agricultural terraces. The figure in relief is Aiapaec, the Andean Water God of the Moche people
Moche ceramic sculpture

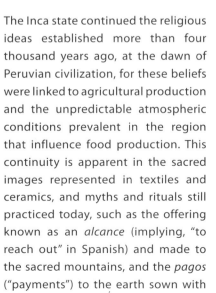

The Inca state continued the religious ideas established more than four thousand years ago, at the dawn of Peruvian civilization, for these beliefs were linked to agricultural production and the unpredictable atmospheric conditions prevalent in the region that influence food production. This continuity is apparent in the sacred images represented in textiles and ceramics, and myths and rituals still practiced today, such as the offering known as an *alcance* (implying, "to reach out" in Spanish) and made to the sacred mountains, and the *pagos* ("payments") to the earth sown with crops. At the head of the pantheon of gods there stood a divine couple, upon whom the success of the harvest depended. They were the God of Water and the Earth Goddess.

In the Inca state, the God of Water was known by a variety of names. Studies have shown the author that the Sun was no other than the personification of the God of Water, however incongruous that may seem. He was seen as a demonic being who controlled the weather according to his whim. This is clear from artistic representations, particularly in the Chavín and Moche cultures, where he is shown with menacing fangs and as an executioner thirsty for human sacrifice.

This god would only show his benevolent side in return for the rituals and sacrifices it was imagined he required (Kauffmann Doig 1996a, 2001a, 2003b). He was offered seashells and llama foetuses or llama fat, as well as children in years of famine when the rains failed and frosts devastated crops. His most commonly repeated emblem was the crest of a wave. The Earth Goddess, or *Pachamama*, was the provider of sustenance as long as she was properly fertilized by the rains the God of Water, her consort, let fall upon her.

(1) Collecting of surplus crops as tribute to the state. (2) An inventory is made of foodstuffs, which are then stored for the years when crops fail. (3) Divine powers had no jurisdiction over morals, which were an affair of state, and offenders were severely punished
Guaman Poma c.1600

The state was exclusively responsible for ensuring that moral codes were not transgressed, such as theft and laziness, as well as for inflicting punishment on offenders. The Andean gods were "gods of sustenance". The God of Water dwelled in the high peaks, or *Apus*, which are still worshipped today. Religious festivities and times of rest and rejoicing occurred on a monthly basis, following the cycles of the agricultural calendar. Viracocha (wira = fat and kotsha = water) seems to have been a mythical version of the God of Water. The bubbles formed by waves on the seashore were seen as the water's fat: its vital essence.

The belief in a life after death like that lived in this world spawned elaborate rituals and tombs which were often monumental, such as the *chullpas* (tshuilipa) of Sillustani. The bodies of the deceased were mummified, for it was believed that life beyond the grave depended on the conservation of the corpse.

Inca society was divided into two classes: the nobility and the people. Apart from a few individuals who distinguished themselves in warfare, a change of status was impossible. Several myths underpinned the belief that the people and the nobility were created unequal by divine will. The nobility was made up of the sovereign, his closest relatives, the members of the high nobility from the provinces incorporated into the Inca state and the priesthood. The sovereign, or *Inca*, wore symbolic emblems and was carried on a litter amid great ceremony. The mass of peasants formed the population of the Inca state. They paid tribute in the form of foodstuffs which were stored for use when crops failed due to unfavourable weather conditions. In addition, specialist workers such as artists and artisans, engineers, architects or state officials consumed a part of the surplus not destined for storage. The tax paying people enjoyed a form of social security, payable in products and services, which exoner-

ated the old or infirm from service to the state. Unlike the nobility, commoners were only permitted to take one wife, and could not marry a close relative. The sovereign, on the other hand, married his sister and kept innumerable concubines. Adultery was punishable, sometimes even by death. Punishments for other offences differed, depending on whether the offender was a noble or a commoner. The *yanaconas* (ianakuna) were a hereditary class of virtual slaves. Education beyond the family was reserved for young nobles.

In terms of artistic expression, the Inca state inherited an ancient and rich Andean tradition. Images captured on textiles and pottery allude to a world of magical-religious beliefs, represented by beautiful symbolic figures. The Inca state's greatest achievement, however, was its architecture, and Machu Picchu is perhaps the most eloquent example of the high level of skill the Incas attained in the art of construction.

Works Consulted

AGURTO CALVO (Santiago)
1986   "Una carta sobre la albañilería incaica". *El Comercio* (9/IX). Lima.
1987   *Estudios acerca de la construcción, arquitectura y planeamientos incas* (Cámara Peruana de la Construcción – CAPECO). Lima.

ALEGRÍA SÁNCHEZ (Richard)
2001   "Wiñay Wayna: causas de la inestabilidad de estructuras inka". *Visión Cultural* (Instituto Nacional de Cultura – Cusco) 4, pp. 117-123. Cusco.

ALTAMIRANO SJ. (Diego Francisco)
c.1700 "El suplicio del primer Túpac Amaru / fragmentos de la Historia del Perú del Padre Diego Francisco Altamirano". *Revista Histórica* 15 (1-2), pp. 143-183. Lima 1942. MS.

ANGLES VARGAS (Víctor)
1972   *Machupijchu / enigmática ciudad inka*. Lima.
2002   *Machu Picchu and the Inca Road y el camino inca*. Lima.

ANÓNIMO – 1539 (¿Miguel de Estete?)
1539   "Relación del sitio del Cusco y principio de las guerras civiles del Perú hasta la muerte de Diego de Almagro / 1535 – 1539". *Colección de Libros y Documentos referentes a la Historia del Perú* 10 (segunda serie), pp. 1-133 / Lima 1934. MS. Cuzco.

ARANÍBAR (Carlos)
1970   "Notas sobre la necropompa entre los Incas". *Revista del Museo Nacional* 36 (1969-1970), pp. 108-142. Lima.

ARÁOZ BECERRA (Hernán)
2001   "Nota en torno a la autenticidad y a la intangibilidad del patrimonio cultural". *Visión Cultural* (Instituto Nacional de Cultura – Cusco) 4, pp. 159-161. Cusco.

ARDILES NIEVES (Percy)
1990   "Camino Inca: Machu Picchu". *Saqsaywaman* (Instituto Departamental de Cultura / Cusco) 3, pp. 143-159. Cusco.

ASTETE (Fernando)
2001   "Aportes e investigaciones en Machu Picchu (1994-2000)". *90 Años del Descubrimiento Científico de Machu Picchu (1994-2000)*. (Instituto Nacional de Cultura, ed. Ernesto Vargas). Cusco.

ASTETE (Fernando) y Rubén ORELLANA
1988   Informe Final 1987: restauración andenes Mandor, Putukusi y aledaños – Machupicchu (Instituto Nacional de Cultura - Cusco). MS.

BARREDA MURILLO (Luis)
2001   "Rumbo al rescate del testimonio arqueológico de Machupiqcho". *Visión Cultural* (Instituto Nacional de Cultura - Cusco) 4, pp. 162-163. Cusco.

BAUER (Brian S.)
1992   *Avances en arqueología andina* (Traducido por Javier Flores Espinoza) / Centro de Estudios Regionales Andinos "Bartolomé de las Casas". Cusco.

BENAVENTE VELÁSQUEZ (Ruperto)
2001   "Evaluación geológica de la ciudadela de Machupicchu". *Visión Cultural* (Instituto Nacional de Cultura – Cusco) 4, pp. 136-141. Cusco.

BENGTSSON (Lisbet)
1998   *Prehistoric Stonework in the Peruvian Andes / A Case Study at Ollantaytambo* (Etnologiska studier 44). Göteborg.

BERGER (Rainer) et al.
1988   "Radiocarbon Dating Machu Picchu, Peru". *Antiquity* 62 (237), pp. 707-710.

BETANZOS (Juan D.)
1551   *Suma y narración de los Incas. Seguida*
-56   *del Discurso sobre la Descendencia y Gobierno de los Incas* (Edición, introducción y notas: María del Carmen Martín Rubio / "Desde la otra orilla": José Carlos Vilcapoma. Madrid 2004). MS.

BINGHAM (Alfred)
1987   "Raiders of the Lost City". *American Heritage* 38 (5), pp. 54-64.
1989   *Portrait of an Explorer: Hiram Bingham, Discoverer of Machu Picchu / Memoir by his son Alfred which contains invaluable personal details about Bingham and the work of the Yale Peruvian expeditions* (Iowa State University Press). Ames.

BINGHAM (Hiram)
1910   "The Ruins of Choqquequirau". *American Anthropologist* 12, pp. 502-525. Lancaster.
1912a   "A Search for the Lost Inca Capital". *Harper's Magazine* 125, pp. 696-705.
1912b   "Vitcos, The Last Inca Capital". *Proceedings of the American Antiquarian Society* 22, pp. 135-196.
1913   "The Discovery of Machu Picchu". *Harper's Magazine* 127, pp. 708-719.
1914   "The Ruins of Espiritupampa". *American Anthropologist* 16 (2), pp. 185-199. Lancaster.
1915a   "The Story of Machu Picchu". *National Geographic Magazine* 27, pp. 172-217. Washington.
1915b   "Types of Machu Picchu Pottery". *American Anthropologist* 17 (2), pp. 257-271.
1930   *Machu Picchu / A Citadel of the Incas* (Yale University Press and Oxford University Press). New Haven.
1948   *Lost City of the Incas / The Story of Machu Picchu and its Builders*. New York.
1949   *La ciudad perdida de los incas (Lost City of the Incas) / Historia de Machu Picchu y sus constructores* [Traducción del inglés publ. en 1948 / Seg. Ed. Empresa Editora Zig-Zag, S.A., Santiago 1953]. Santiago

2002   *Lost City of the Incas / The Story of Machu Picchu and its Builders* (With an introduction by Hugh Thomson / Photographs by Hugh Thomson). London.

BONAVIA (Duccio)
1997   "Muros poligonales incaicos". *Arkinka* 15, pp. 102-108. Lima.
1999   "La cantera incaica". *Arkinka* 42, pp. 90-99. Lima.

BOUCHARD (Jean-François)
1991   "La arquitectura inca". *Los incas y el antiguo Perú / 3000 años de historia* 1, pp. 434-453. Madrid.

BOUCHARD (J.-F.), CARLOTTO (V.) y P. USSELMAN
1992   "Machu Picchu: problemas de conservación de un sitio inca de ceja de selva". *Bulletin de l'Institut Française d'Études Andines* 21 (3), pp. 905-927. Lima.

BUCK (Daniel)
1993   "Fights of Machu Picchu". *South American Explorer* 32, pp. 22-32.

BUENO (Cosme)
c.1786 *Geografía del Perú virreinal* (Publicado por Carlos Daniel Valcárcel. Universidad Nacional Mayor de San Marcos / Lima 1951).

BURGER (Richard L.)
2004   "Scientific insights into daily life at Machu Picchu". *Machu Picchu - unveiling the mystery of the Incas* / Edited by Richard L. Burger and Lucy C. Salazar (Yale University Press), pp. 85-106. New Haven and London.

BURGER (Richard L.) y Lucy SALAZAR
1993   "Machu Picchu Rediscovered: The royal estate in the cloud forest". *Discovery* 24 (2), pp. 20-25.

BURGER (Richard L.) y Lucy C. SALAZAR, eds.
2003   *The 1912 Yale Peruvian scientic expedition collections from Machu Picchu / Human and animal remains.* (Yale University Publications in Anthropology 85). New Haven, Connecticut.
2004   *Machu Picchu - unvelling the mystery of the incas* (Yale University Press). New Haven and London.

BUSE (Hermann)
1961   *Machupicchu*. Lima.
1978   *Machu Picchu*. Lima.

CABADA (Eulogio)
1983   "Arquitectura de las construcciones del grupo de las tres ventanas en la ciudadela de Machupicchu". *Revista del Museo e Instituto de Arqueología* 20, pp. 79-114, Cusco.

CABIESES (Fernando)
1983   *Machu Picchu / una ciudad sagrada (apuntes etnohistóricos de Fernando Cabieses)*. Lima.

CALANCHA (Antonio de la)
1638   *Coronica moralizada de la orden de San Augustin en el Perú, con sucesos egenplares en*

esta monarquia. Dedicada a Nuestra Señora de Gracia, singular patrona i abogada de la dicha orden. Compuesta por el muy reverendo padre maestro Fray Antonio de la Calancha de la misma orden, i definidor actual. Divídese este primer tomo en quatro libros; lleva tablas de capítulos, i lugares de la sagrada escritura. Año 1638. Con licencia. En Barcelona: Por Pedro Lacavalleria, en la calle de la Librería. Barcelona.

CAMACHO PAREDES (Darwin)
(2004)   *The True History of Machupicchu.* Cusco.

CARLOTTO CAILLAUX (Víctor) y José CÁRDENAS ROQUE
2001   "La geología, los problemas de conservación e impacto ambiental en el Santuario Histórico de Machu Picchu". *Visión Cultural* (Instituto Nacional de Cultura – Cusco) 4, pp. 129-35. Cusco.

CHÁVEZ BALLÓN (Manuel)
1955   "Tipos de cerámica de Machu Picchu". *Tradición* 7, pp. 7-10. Cusco.
1961   "La alfarería de Machupicchu". *Revista del Museo e Instituto Arqueológico* 19, pp. 182-196. Cuzco.
1971   "Trabajos de limpieza, conservación, restauración e investigación en Machupijchu y el museo". *Visión Cultural* (Instituto Nacional de Cultura – Cusco) 4, pp. 67-92. Cusco 2001 / MS.

CHEVARRÍA HUARCAYA (Efraín)
1992   *Machupicchu / devenir histórico y cultural* (Editorial, selección y notas Efraín Chevarría Huarcaya / Universidad Nacional San Antonio Abad del Cusco). Cusco.

CHRISTENSEN (Eric)
2002   *Machu Picchu: Orchids / Machu Picchu: orquídeas.* Lima.

CIEZA DE LEÓN (Pedro)
c.1550   *El señorío de los incas / Segunda parte de la Crónica del Perú.* (Introducción de Carlos Araníbar / Instituto de Estudios Peruanos. Lima 1967). MS.
1553   *Parte primera de la choronica del Peru: Que tracta la demarcacion de sus prouincias; la descripcion dellas. Las fundaciones de las nueuas ciudades. Los ritos y costumbres de los indios. Y cosas estrañas dignas de ser sabidas. Fecha por Pedro Cieça de Leon vezino de Seuilla.* ("Crónica del Perú / Primera Parte": Introducción de Franklin Pease G.Y. Notas de Miguel Maticorena E. / Pontificia Universidad Católica del Perú. Lima 1986). Sevilla.

COBO (Bernabé)
c.1653   *Historia del nuevo mundo* (Biblioteca de autores españoles desde la formación del lenguaje hasta nuestros días: Obras del P. Bernabé Cobo de la Compañía de Jesús, 2 vs. Madrid 1956). MS.

COOK (O.F.)
1916   "Staircase Faros of the Ancients". *National Geographic Magazine* May, pp. 474-534. Washington.

CORNEJO BOURONCLE (Jorge)
1961   "Machupicchu". *Revista del Museo e Instituto Arqueológico* 19, pp. 154-165. Cusco.

COSIO (José Gabriel)
1912   "Machupiccho / ciudad preincaica en el valle del Vilcanota". *Boletín de la Sociedad Geográfica de Lima* 28, pp. 147-161. Lima.

1951   "Vitcos, la última capital de los incas". *Revista del Museo e Instituto Arqueológico* 13-14, pp. 4-17. Cuzco.
1961   *Informe elevado al Ministerio de Instrucción por el doctor don José Gabriel Cosío, delegado del Supremo Gobierno y de la Sociedad Geográfica de Lima, ante la Comisión Científica de 1912 enviada por la Universidad de Yale y la National Geographic Society de Washington, acerca de los trabajos realizados por ella en el Cuzco y Apurímac. Revista del Museo e Instituto Arqueológico* (Universidad del Cuzco) 19, pp. 326-364. Cuzco.

DEARBORN (David S.P.), SCHREIBER (Katharina J.) y Raymond E. WHITE
1987   "Intimachay: a December Solstice Observatory at Machu Picchu, Peru". *American Antiquity* 52 (2), pp. 346-352.

DEL VALLE CHOUSA (Santiago)
2005   *El misterio de Vilcabamba / el hallazgo de la capital perdida.* Coruña.

EATON (George F.)
1916   "The collection of osteological material from Machu Picchu". *Memoirs of the Connecticut Academy of Arts and Sciences* 5. New Haven.
1990   *La colección del material osteológico de Machu Picchu* (New Haven, Connecticut 1916 / Traducción de Sonia Guillén). Lima.

ELORRIETA SALAZAR (Fernando E.) y Edgar ELORRIETA SALAZAR
1996   *El valle sagrado de los incas / mitos y símbolos.* Cusco.

ESPINOZA SORIANO (Waldemar)
1967   "Los señoríos étnicos de Chachapoyas y la alianza hispano-chacha". *Revista Histórica* 30, pp. 224-332. Lima.

ESQUIVEL Y NAVIA (Diego de)
c.1750   *Noticias cronológicas de la gran ciudad del Cuzco* (Edición, prólogo y notas de Félix Denegri Luna con la colaboración de Horacio Villanueva Urteaga y César Gutiérrez Muñoz) 2 vs. Lima 1980) MS.

FEJOS (Paul)
1944   *Archaeological Explorations in the Cordillera Vilcabamba, Peru* (Viking Foundation / Publication 3). New York.

FLORES OCHOA (Jorge A.)
2004   "Contemporary Significance of Machu Picchu". *Machu Picchu - unveiling the mystery of the incas* / Edited by Richard L. Burger and Lucy C. Salazar (Yale University Press), pp. 109-123. New Haven and London.

FROST (Peter)
1989   *Exploring Cusco* (4th Edition). Lima.

FROST (Peter) et al. - Jim BARTLE
1995   *Santuario Histórico Machu Picchu / Cusco, Perú.* Lima.

FROST (Peter) – Fotografías de Gordon Wiltsie
2004   "La misteriosa montaña de los incas". *National Geographic* / en español 14 (2), pp. 48-63.

GALLEGOS (Héctor)
2000   *El viejo Perú* (Colección: La Ingeniería en el Perú). Lima.

GARCÍA (José Uriel)
1961a   "Machu Picchu". *Cuadernos Americanos* 117 (4). México.

1961b   "Machu-Picchu / un centro de trabajo femenino / documento de piedra para la historia de los incas". *Visión Cultural* (Instituto Nacional de Cultura – Cusco) 4, pp. 24-66. Cusco 2001. MS.

GARCILASO DE LA VEGA (Inca)
1609   *Primera parte de los comentarios reales, que tratan del origen de los yncas, reyes qve fueron del Perv, de sv idolatría, leyes, y govierno en paz y en guerra: de sus vidas y conquistas, y de todo lo que fue aquel imperio y su república, antes que los españoles passaran a el. Escritos Por el ynca Garcilasso de la Vega, natural del Cozco, y capitan de su majestad. Dirigidos a la serenísima princesa doña Catalina de Portugal, duqueza de Barganza, &c* (Emecé Editores S.A. Buenos Aires 1943). Lisboa.

GASPARINI (Graziano) y Luise MARGOLIES
1977   *Arquitectura inka.* Caracas.
1980   *Inca architecture* (Indiana University Press). Bloomington.

GIBAJA OVIEDO (Arminda M.)
2001   "Aspectos constructivos en Machupicchu". *Visión Cultural* (Instituto Nacional de Cultura – Cusco) 4, pp.107-111. Cusco.

GIESECKE (Albert A.)
1961   "Breves apuntes de la vida y obra de Hiram Bingham". *Revista del Museo e Instituto Arqueológico* (Universidad del Cuzco) 19, pp. 11-25. Cuzco.

GLAVE (Luis Miguel) y María Isabel REMY
1983   *Estructura agraria y vida rural en una región andina / Ollantaytambo entre los siglos XVI-XIX.* (Centro de Estudios Rurales Andinos "Bartolomé de las Casas / Archivos de Historia Andina 3). Cusco.

GOFF (Charles W.)
1966   "The Tombs of Machu Picchu". *Americas*, vol. 18, nº 8, pp. 8-18. Washington.

GÖHRING (Herman)
1877   *Informe al supremo gobierno del Perú sobre la expedición a los valles de Paucartambo en 1873, al mando del coronel d. Baltasar La Torre.* Lima.

GONÇALEZ HOLGUIN (Diego)
1608   *Vocabulario de la lengua general de todo el Perú llamada lengua qquichua o del Inca [...].* Impreso en la Ciudad de los Reyes (Reed. Lima 1952). Lima.

GONZÁLEZ (Elena) y Rafael LEON (Editores)
2001   *Machu Picchu: Santuario Histórico / Historical Sanctuary* (Fotografías de Jorge H. Esquiroz). AFP INTEGRA. Lima.

GORDON (Robert B.)
1986   "Metallurgy of Bronze Tools from Machu Picchu" *Proceedings of the 24th International Archaeometry Symposium* (Smithsonian Institution), pp. 233-242. Washington D.C.

GUAMAN POMA DE AYALA (Phelipe)
c.1600   *Nueva coronica y buen gobierno* (París 1936). Lima.

GUILLÉN GUILLÉN (Edmundo)
1974   *Versión inca de la conquista.* Lima.
1977   "Vilcabamba: la última capital del Estado imperial inca". *Scientia et Praxis* 1. Lima.
1978   "Documentos inéditos para la historia de los Incas de Vilcabamba: la capitulación del gobierno español con Titu Cusi Yupanqui". *Historia y Cultura* (Museo Nacional de Historia) 10, pp. 47-93. Lima.

1981 "Titu Cusi Yupanqui y su tiempo / el estado imperial inka y su trágico final: 1572". *Historia y Cultura* 13-14, pp. 61-99. Lima.

1984 "Tres documentos inéditos para la historia de la guerra de reconquista inca". *Boletín del Instituto Francés de Estudios Andinos* 19 (1-2), pp. 17-46. Lima.

1994 *La guerra de la reconquista inka.* Lima.

HARTH-TERRÉ (Emilio)

1961 "El urbanismo en el antiguo Perú / Machu-Picchu ciudad antártica". *Revista del Museo e Instituto Arqueológico* 19, pp. 165-177. Cuzco.

1965 "Técnica y arte de la cantería incaica". *Revista Universitaria* (Universidad Nacional del Cuzco) 122-123, 124-125 (1962-1963). Cuzco.

HEMMING (John)

1970 *The Conquest of the Incas.* London.

HUAYCOCHEA NÚÑEZ DE LA TORRE (Flor de María)

1994 *Qolqas / bancos de reserva andinos / almacenes inkas / arqueología de qolqas.* Cusco.

HYSLOP (John)

1992 *Qhapaqñan / el sistema vial inkaico.* Lima.

INRENA (Instituto Nacional de Recursos Naturales)

1999 *Plan maestro del Santuario Histórico de Machupicchu.* Lima.

INSTITUTO NACIONAL DE CULTURA (LIMA) / INSTITUTO NACIONAL DE CULTURA (CUSCO)

2005 *Plan Maestro del Santuario Histórico de Machu Picchu - Resumen.* Lima.

INSTITUTO NACIONAL DE RECURSOS NATURALES (INRENA)

1999 *Plan Maestro del Santuario Histórico de Machu Picchu.* Lima.

KALAFATOVICH VALLE (Carlos)

1963 "Geología de la ciudadela de Machu Picchu y sus alrededores". *Revista Universitaria* (Universidad Nacional San Antonio de Abad) 121, pp. 217-228. Cuzco.

KARP DE TOLEDO (Eliane)

2004a "El turismo y el desarrollo de los pueblos indígenas". *La diversidad cultural y los ciudadanos del Sol y la Luna / Proyectos para la inclusión social y el desarrollo con identidad de los pueblos originarios del Perú,* pp. 47-57. Lima.

2004b "Machu Picchu y la peruanidad responsable". *La diversidad cultural y los ciudadanos del Sol y la Luna / Proyectos para la inclusión social y el desarrollo con identidad de los pueblos originarios del Perú,* pp. 143-155. Lima.

KAUFFMANN DOIG (Federico)

1965 "Lo inca en la arquitectura colonial: el fenómeno huamanquino". *La Universidad y el Pueblo* / Segunda época (Universidad Nacional Mayor de San Marcos) 3, pp. 108-183. Lima.

1985 "Arquitectura zoomorfa: la ciudad del Cusco, con anotaciones acerca de la arquitectura e iconografía Chavín". *Boletín de Lima* 38, pp. 27-34. Lima.

1986a "Los dioses andinos / hacia una caracterización de la religiosidad fundamentada en testimonios arqueológicos y en mitos". *Revista EV / Vida y Espiritualidad* 3, pp. 1-16. Lima.

1986b "Sarcófagos pre-incas en los Andes Amazónicos". *Kuntur / Perú en la cultura* 1, pp. 4-9. Lima.

1991a *Introducción al Perú antiguo* (Primera edición 1990). Lima.

1991b "Sobrepoblación en los Andes / una explicación del origen y proceso de la cultura andina". *L'imaginaire* (Alianza Francesa) 3, pp. 45-48. Lima.

1996a "Gestación y rostro de la civilización andina". *Lienzo* (Revista de la Universidad de Lima) 17, pp. 9-55. Lima.

1996b "Los Andes Amazónicos y su pasado arqueológico". *Política Internacional* (Revista de la Academia Diplomática del Perú) 46, pp. 113-143. Lima.

2001a "Hiram Bingham y la historia de Machu Picchu". *Perú Contemporáneo* (Revista de Historia y Sociedad) 2, pp. 153-166. Lima.

2001b "Machu Picchu en riesgo". *El Comercio* (15-III). Lima.

2001c "Religión andina". *Enciclopedia Ilustrada del Perú* 14, pp. 231-232. Lima.

2001d *Sexo y magia sexual en el antiguo Perú / Sex and Sexual Magic in Ancient Peru.* Lima.

2002 *Historia y arte del Perú antiguo,* 6 vols. Lima.

2003a "Andean Gods: Gods of sustenance". *Precolombart* 4/5 (2001-2002), pp. 55-69. Barcelona.

2003b "Los dioses andinos: dioses del sustento". *Precolombart* 4-5 (2001-2002), pp. 55-69. Barcelona.

KAUFFMANN DOIG (Federico) y Giancarlo LIGABUE

2003 *Los chachapoya(s) / moradores de los Andes Amazónicos Peruanos* (Universidad Alas Peruanas). Lima.

KENDALL (Ann)

1969 "The Temple of the Moon, Machu Picchu". *Peruvian Times* (14-X). Lima.

1974 "Architecture and planning at the Inca sites in the Cusichaca area". *Baessler-Archiv* (Neue Folge) 22, pp. 73-137. Berlin.

1978 "Descripción e inventario de las formas arquitectónicas inca. Patrones de distribución e inferencias cronológicas". *Revista del Museo Nacional* 42 (1976), pp. 13-96. Lima.

1988 "Inca planning north of Cuzco between Anta and Machu Picchu and along the Urubamba valley". *Recent Studies in Pre-Columbian Archaeology* / BAR / International Series 421, pp. 457-388. Oxford.

KOSOK (Paul)

1965 *Land, life and water in ancient Peru.* (Long Island University Press). New York

KUBLER (George)

1947 "The Neo-Inca State (1537-1572)". *The Hispanic American Historical Review* 24, pp. 253-276.

LACERTE (Dominique R.)

2000 *The biographies of the members of the 1911 Yale Peruvian Expedition and the Peruvian Expedition of 1912 under the auspices of the Yale University and the National Geographic Society* (Tesis universitaria / Yale University, Archaeological Studies Program). MS.

LARREA (Juan)

1961 "Machupicchu / ciudad de la última esperanza. *Revista del Museo e Instituto de Arqueología* 19, pp. 299-235. Cuzco.

LAVANDAIS (Eugenio de) / ps. Vizconde de Sartiges

1834 *Dos viajeros franceses en el Perú* (Edición, prólogo y notas Raúl Porras Barrenechea, Lima 1947 / Originalmente publ. en *La Revue des deux Mondes* 851, pp. 1019 y sigtes. MS.

LEE (Vincent R.)

1985 *Sixpac Manco: Travels Among the Incas.* Wyoming.

1989 *Chanasuyo / The Ruins of Inca Vilcabamba (…).* Wyoming.

2000 *Forgotten Vilcabamba / Final Stronghold of the Incas* (Sixpac Manco Publications). Wyoming.

LEÓN (Rafael) et al.

2000 *El camino a Machu Picchu / la aventura de la historia.* Lima.

LOHMANN VILLENA (Guillermo)

1941 "El Inca Titu Cusi Yupanqui y su entrevista con el oidor Matienzo 1565". *Mercurio Peruano* 166, pp. 2-18. Lima.

LÓPEZ LENCI (Yazmín)

2004 *El Cusco, paqarina moderna / cartografía de una modernidad e identidades en los andes peruanos (1900-1935)* (Universidad Nacional Mayor de San Marcos). Lima.

LUMBRERAS (Luis G.) y Walter WUST

2001 *Choquequirao, santuario histórico y ecológico.* Lima.

MACKEHENIE (Carlos A.)

1908 "Apuntes sobre don Diego de Castro Titu
-13 Cusi Yupanqui". *Revista Histórica* 3 (4), pp. 371-390 y 5 (1), pp. 5-14. Lima.

MARKHAM (Clements R.)

1856 *Cuzco/A Journey to the Ancient Capital of Peru.* London.

MARTÍNEZ (Antonio)

1999 "Cusco misterioso. Choquesuysuy: el Camino de la Purificación / The Purification Trail". *Rumbos de Sol & Piedra* 16, pp. 23-31. Lima.

MARTÍN RUBIO (María del Carmen)

1988 "Los Incas de Vilcabamba". *Encuentro de dos mundos.* Madrid.

2004 Véase BETANZOS 1551-56.

MATHENWSON (C.H.)

1915 "A metallographic description of some ancient Peruvian bronzes from Machu Picchu". *American Journal of Science* 40, pp. 525-616.

MATIENZO (Juan de)

1567 *Gobierno del Perú* (Edición y estudio preliminares por Guillermo Lohmann Villena / Instituto Francés de Estudios Andinos). París-Lima.

MIDDENDORF (Ernst W.)

1890 *Die einheimischen Sprachen Perus.* 6 vs.
-92 Leipzig.

MILLER (Georg R.)

2003 "Food for the dead, tools for the afterlife. Zooarchaeology at Machu Picchu". *The 1912 Yale Peruvian Scientific Expedition Collections from Machu Picchu. Human Remains* / Richard L. Burger, Lucy Salazar, Editors (Yale University Publications in Anthropology) 85, pp. 1-63. New Haven.

MILLONES (Luis)

Véase: TITU CUSI YUPANQUI 1570

MOHR-CHÁVEZ (Karen L.)

1980 "The Archaeology of Marcavalle / An early horizon site in the valley of Cusco, Peru". *Baessler Archiv* (Neue Folge) 28, pp. 203-329. Berlín.

MORRIS (E. Craig)

1967 *Storage in Tawantinsuyo* (Tesis Doctoral / Universidad de Chicago, Illinois). Chicago.

MOULD de PEASE (Mariana)
2003 *Machu Picchu y el código de ética de la Sociedad de Arqueología Americana.* Lima.

MUELLE (Jorge C.)
1945 "Pacarectambo: apuntes de viaje". *Revista del Museo Nacional* 14, pp. 153-160. Lima.

MUELLE (Jorge C.); BONAVIA (Duccio); RAVINES S. (Rogger) y Manuel CHÁVEZ BALLÓN
1972 "Delimitación del área intangible de Machu Picchu". *Visión Cultural* (Instituto Nacional de Cultura – Cusco) 4, pp. 93-95. Cusco 2001. MS.

MURÚA (Martín de)
c.1600 *Historia general del Perú y origen y descendencia de los reyes Yncas* (Manuel Ballesteros-Gaibrois: Colección Joyas Bibliográficas / Biblioteca Americana Vetus, 2 vs. Madrid 1962-1964). MS.

NECOCHEA (Carlos) y Bernabé CALDERÓN
2001 "El imperio se mantiene sólido / macizo de granito impide que Machu Picchu se desmorone". *El Comercio* (26-III). Lima.

NILES (Susan A.)
2004 "The Nature of Inca Royal States. *Machu Picchu / unveiling the mystery of the Incas* / Edited by Richard L. Burger and Lucy C. Salazar (Yale University Press), pp. 49-68. New Haven and London.

OCAMPO CONEJEROS (Baltazar)
c.1611 "Descripción y sucesos históricos de la provincia de Vilcabamba, por […]". *Juicio de Límites entre el Perú y Bolivia / Prueba Peruana presentada al Gobierno de la República Argentina por Víctor M Martua Abogado y Plenipotenciario del Perú 7*, pp. 306-344. (Lima 1906). Barcelona

ORICAIN (Pablo José)
1790 "Compendio breve de los discursos varios sobre diferentes materias y noticias geográficas comprehensivas a este obispado del Cusco". Víctor M Maurtua: *Juicio de Límites entre Perú y Bolivia 2*, pp. 321-37. Barcelona (1906). MS.

ORTIZ RESCANIER (Alejandro)
1973 *De Adaneva a Inkarrí / Una visión indígena del Perú.* Lima.

PACHACUTI YAMQUI SALCAMAYGUA (Joan de Santa Cruz)
1627(?) *Relación de antigüedades desde reyno del Piru* (Estudio Etnohistórico y Lingüístico de Pierre Duviols y César Itier / Edición facsimilar y transcripción paleográfica del Códice de Madrid - Cusco 1993). MS.

PARDO (Luis A.)
1946 "La metrópoli de Paccarictambu: el adoratorio de Tamputtocco y el itinerario del camino seguido por los hermanos Ayar". *Revista del Instituto Arqueológico del Cusco 2*, pp. 2-46. Cusco.
1961a "Exposición de los trabajos de defensa, consolidación y restauración realizados en Machu Picchu en los últimos veintidós años". *Revista del Museo e Instituto Arqueológico 19*, pp. 197-215. Cuzco.
1961b "Machupicchu (una joya arquitectónica de los incas)". Prólogo de José Gabriel Losio. Revista del Museo e Instituto Arqueológico 19, pp. 223-298. Cuzco.
1972 *El imperio de Vilcabamba / el reinado de los cuatro últimos incas* (Con colofón de Alfredo Yépez Miranda). Cusco.

PIZARRO (Pedro)
1571 *Relación del descubrimiento y conquista de los reinos del Perú* (Buenos aires 1944). MS.

PROTZEN (Jean-Pierre)
1983 "Inca quarrying and stonecutting". *Ñawpa Pacha* (Institute of Andean Studies) 21, pp. 183-214. Berkeley, California.
1985 "Inca quarrying and stonecutting". *Journal of the Society of Architectural Historians* 44 (2), pp. 161-182.
1986 "Inca stonemasonry". *Scientific American* 254 (11), pp. 80-88. New York.

RAIMONDI, Antonio
1874- *El Perú.* 6 vs. Lima.
1913

REGALADO DE HURTADO (Liliana)
1981 "La Relación de Titu Kusi Yupanqui, valor de un testimonio". *Histórica* 5 (1), pp. 45-61. Lima.
1992 *Religión y evangelización en Vilcabamba / 1572-1622.* Lima.
1997 *El inca Titu Cusi Yupanqui y su tiempo.* Lima.

REINHARD (Johan)
1991 *Machu Picchu / The Sacred Center.* Lima.
2002a *Machu Picchu / centro sagrado* (Instituto Machu Picchu / coordinador editorial Jim Bartle / Traductor responsable Walter Wust). Lima.
2002b *Machu Picchu / The Sacred Center* (Published by Instituto Machu Picchu / Editorial coordinator Jim Bartle). Lima.

RIVEROS CAYO (Jorge)
2004 "Un mito llamado Hiram Bingham". *Arkinka* 101, pp. 92-99. Lima.

ROCHA (Álvaro)
2004 "Viajes. Nueva ruta para arribar a Machu Picchu / el otro sendero". Somos 930, pp. 49-55. Lima

RODRÍGUEZ DE FIGUEROA (Diego)
1565 *Relación del camino e viaje que Diego Rodríguez hizo desde la ciudad del Cuzco a la tierra de guerra de Manco Inga, que está en los Andes alzado contra el servicio de S. M, y de las cosas que con él trató, por modo y manera de paz y también para que recibiese la doctrina evangélica de N. S. Jesucristo.* (Colección de Libros y Documentos referentes a la Historia del Perú 1ª serie, 2. Lima 1916 / Primera edición: Richard Pietschmann, 1910). MS.

ROMERO (Carlos A.)
1909 "Informe del señor Carlos A. Romero, individuo de número del Instituto, sobre las ruinas de Choqquequirau". *Revista Histórica* (Órgano del Instituto Histórico del Perú) 4, pp. 87-103. Lima.

ROSTWOROWSKI (María)
1963 "Dos manuscritos inéditos con datos sobre Manco II / tierras personales de los incas y mitmaes". *Nueva Coronica* 1, pp. 223-239. Lima.
1970 "El repartimiento de doña Beatriz Coya en el valle de Yucay". *Historia y Cultura* (Museo Nacional de Historia) 4, pp. 153-267. Lima.

ROWE (John H.)
1946 "Inca culture at the time of the Spanish conquest. *Handbook of South American Indians* 2, pp. 183-330. Washington, D.C.
1967 "What kind of a settlement was Inca Cuzco?". *Ñawpa Pacha* (Institute of Andean Studies) 5,

pp. 59-76, plate XXXIV. Berkeley, California.
1980 "An account of the shrines of ancient Cusco". *Ñawpa Pacha* (Institute of Andean Studies) 17 (1979), pp. 1-80. Berkeley.
1990 "Machu Pijchu a la luz de documentos del siglo XVI". *Histórica* 14 (1), pp. 139-154. Lima.

RUTLEDGE (John W.) y Robert GORDON
1987 "The work of metallurgical artificers at Machu Picchu, Peru". *American Antiquity* 52 (3), pp. 578-594.

SALAZAR (Lucy C.)
2004 "Machu Picchu: mysterious royal estate in the cloud forest". *Machu Picchu / unveiling the mystery of the Incas* / Edited by Richard L. Burger and Lucy C. Salazar (Yale University Press), pp. 21-47. New Haven and London.

SALAZAR (Lucy C.) y Richard L. BURGER
2004 "Catalogue" *Machu Picchu / unveiling the mystery of the Incas* (Edited by Richard L. Burger and Lucy C. Salazar / Yale University Press), pp. 124-217. New Haven and London.

SAMANEZ (Roberto) y Julinho ZAPATA
1996 "El templo del sol en Vilcabamba". *Arkinka* 2, pp. 62-72. Lima.

SÁNCHEZ MACEDO (Marino)
1990 "De las sacerdotisas, brujas y adivinas de Machupicchu". Cusco.

SAN ROMÁN LUNA (Wilbert)
2001 "Las restauraciones en la ciudad inka de Machupicchu / 1985, 1987". *Visión Cultural* (Instituto Nacional de Cultura – Cusco) 4, pp. 112-115.Cusco.

SAVOY (Gene)
1964 "Discovery of the Ruins of Vilcabamba". *Peruvian Times* (9 / IV). Lima.
1970 *Antisuyo / The Search for the Lost Cities of the Amazon.* New York.

SHADY SOLÍS (Ruth M.)
1997 *La ciudad sagrada de Caral-Supe en los albores de la civilización en el Perú* (Universidad Nacional Mayor de San Marcos). Lima.

SQUIER (E. George)
1877 *Perú / Incidents of Travel and Exploration in the Land of the Incas.* New York.

TAYPE RAMOS (Pablo Vidal)
2001 Véase NECOCHEA y CALDERÓN 2001

TEMPLE (Ella Dunbar)
1937 "La descendencia de Huayna Cápac".
-48 *Revista Histórica* 11, pp. 93-115; 12, pp. 204-245; 13, pp. 31-77; 17, pp. 134-179. Lima.
1950 El testamento inédito de doña Beatriz Clara Coya de Loyola, hija de Sayri Túpac. *Fénix* (Biblioteca Nacional) 7, pp. 109-122. Lima.

TITU CUSI YUPANQUI (Diego de Castro)
1570 *Ynstruccion del Ynga don Diego de Castro Titu Cussi Yupangui para el muy ilustre señor el licenciado Lope García de Castro, gobernador que fue destos reynos del Piru, tocante a los negocios que con su majestad, en su nombre, por su poder de tratar; la qual es esta que se sigue* (Introducción de Luis Millones / Ediciones El Virrey, Lima 1985). MS.

TORD (Luis Enrique)
1975 *Guide to Machu Picchu / including one plan one map, 8 color plates and 14 photographs* (Introduction Duccio Bonavia). Lima.

UHLE (Max)
1910 "Datos para la explicación de los intihuatanas".

Revista Universitaria (Universidad Nacional Mayor de San Marcos) 5 (1), pp. 325-352. Lima.

URTON (Gary)

1990 *The History of a State Myth: Pacariqtambo and the Origin of the Inkas* (University of Texas Press). Austin.

VALCÁRCEL (Luis E.)

1961 "Sinopsis de Machu Picchu". *Revista del Museo e Instituto de Arqueología* 19, pp. 122-135. Cuzco.

1964 *Machu Picchu el más famoso monumento arqueológico del Perú*. Buenos Aires.

VALENCIA ZEGARRA (Alfredo)

1977 *Excavaciones arqueológicas en Machupijchu: sector de la "Roca Sagrada"* (INC - CRSIRBM). Cusco.

1997 "Machu Picchu / ancient agricultural potencial". *Applied Engineering in Agriculture* 132 (1), pp. 39-47.

2004 "Recent archaeological investigations at Machu Picchu". *Machu Picchu - unveiling the mystery of the Incas* / Edited by Richard L. Burger and Lucy C. Salazar (Yale University Press), pp. 71-82. New Haven and London.

VALENCIA ZEGARRA (Alfredo) y Arminda GIBAJA OVIEDO

1991 *Marcavalle / el rostro oculto del Cusco* (Instituto Regional de Cultura de la Región Inka). Cusco.

1992 *Machupijchu / la investigación y conservación del monumento después de Hiram Bingham* (Municipalidad del Qosqo). Qosqo.

VALLE (Santiago del)

(Del Valle)

VARGAS CALDERÓN (César)

1961 "Homenaje botánico a Machupicchu". *Revista del Museo e Instituto Arqueológico del Cusco* 19, pp. 365-384. Cusco.

1992 "Flora del Santuario Histórico de Machupicchu". *Machu Pichu / devenir histórico y cultural*, pp. 39-77. (Ed.: Efraín CHEVARRÍA HUARCAYA). Cusco.

VARGAS P. (Benito)

2001 "Observación visual fotográfica: Machupicchu a 90 años de su 'descubrimiento científico'". *Visión Cultural* (Instituto Nacional de Cultura – Cusco) 4, pp. 167-172. Cusco.

VARÓN GABAI (Rafael)

1993 "Machu Picchu: nuevos datos para su historia". *El Comercio*, 25-Nov. Lima.

1996 La ilusión de la conquista / apogeo y decadencia de los Pizarro en la conquista del Perú (Instituto de Estudios Peruanos / Instituto Francés de Estudios Andinos). Lima.

VEGA (Juan José)

1963 *La guerra de los viracochas*. Lima.

1964 *Manco Inca*. Lima.

1980 *Incas contra españoles / treinta batallas*. Lima.

2000 *Rodrigo Orgoños / el mariscal judío*. Lima.

VELARDE (Héctor)

1946 *Arquitectura peruana* (Fondo de Cultura Económica). México D.F.

VELARDE (Anthony) y Walter HUPIU

2005 "Caminando de Choquequirao a Machu Picchu / Walking from Choquequirao to Machu Picchu". Rumbos / de Sol y Piedra 43, pp. 60-80. Lima.

VERA HERRERA (Leoncio)

2001 "Kantupata". *Visión Cultural* (Instituto Nacional de Cultura – Cusco) 4, pp.124-125. Cusco.

VERANO (John W.)

2003 "Human skeletal remains from Machu Picchu / A Yale Peabody Museum's Collections". *The 1912 Yale Peruvian Scientific Expedition Collections from Machu Picchu. Human and Animal Remains* / Richard L. Burger, Lucy C. Salazar, Editors (Yale University Publications in Anthropology 85, pp. 65-117). New Haven.

VIDAL (Humberto)

1958 *Visión del Cusco / Monografía sintética*. Cusco

WAVRIN (Marqués de)

1961 "Wayna Picchu / Fragmentos inéditos del libro de viajes del Marqués de Wavrin". *Revista del Museo e Instituto Arqueológico* 19, pp. 136-153. Cuzco.

WHITE (Raymond E.) y David S. P. DEARBORN

1980 *Field report of the Earthwatch expedition "Astronomers of Machu Picchu"* / 14 June – 11 July 1980 (The University of Arizona / Steward Observatory). Tucson.

WIENER (Charles)

1880 *Pérou et Bolivie*. Paris.

WRIGHT (K.R.), KELLY (J.M.) y A. VALENCIA ZEGARRA

1997 "Machu Picchu: Ancient hydraulic engineering". *Journal of Hydraulic Engineering* 123 (10), pp. 838-843.

WRIGHT (K.R.), WITT (G.D.) y A. VALENCIA

1997 "Hydrogeology and Paleohydrology of Ancient Machu Picchu". *Groundwater* 35 (4), pp. 660-666.

WRIGHT (K.R.), WRIGHT (R.M.), JENSEN (M.E.) y A. WRIGHT (K.R.) y R.M. WRIGHT

1997 *Machu Picchu: Its engineering infrastructure.* (The Institute of Andean Studies / 37th Annual Meeting). Berkeley-California.

WRIGHT (K.R.), VALENCIA ZEGARRA (A.) y W.L. LORAH

1999 "Ancient Machu Picchu Drainage Engineering". Journal of Irrigation and Drainage Engineering (Nov.-Dec.).

WRIGHT (K.R.), VALENCIA ZEGARRA (A.) y C. CROWLEY

2000 *Archaeological exploration of the Inca Trail, east flank of Machu Picchu and Palynology of Terraces. Completion report, Instituto de Cultura* / Note: the results of the pollen testing by Linda Scott Cummings are included in this report (Wright Water Engineers and Wright Paleohydrological Institute). Denver.

WRIGHT (Ruth M.) y Alfredo VALENCIA ZEGARRA

2001 *The Machu Picchu Guide Book / A self-guide tour.* Boulder, Colorado.

WURSTER (Wolfgang W.)

2001 "Observaciones acerca de la conservación de monumentos incaicos dentro del parque arqueológico de Machu Picchu". *Visión Cultural* (Instituto Nacional de Cultura – Cusco) 4, pp. 126-128. Cusco.

YÉPEZ VALDÉS (Wilfredo)

2001 "Un intento…, para Machu Picchu". *Visión Cultural* (Instituto Nacional de Cultura – Cusco) 4, pp. 96-102. Cusco.

ZAPATA (Mohemi Julinho)

1983 *Investigación arqueológica en Machu Picchu / Sector Militar* (Tesis de Licenciatura en Antropología / Universidad Nacional San Antonio Abad). Cusco. MS.

ZAPATA VELASCO (Antonio)

1999 *Guía de Machu Picchu* (PROMPERÚ / Serie Turismo 1). Lima.

ZECENARRO BENAVENTE (Germán)

2004 "Saywas y suqanqas, usnus y asientos del Sol / Instrumentos de medición astronómica. *Arkinka* 106, pp. 86-98. Lima.

Glossary

Words in the language of the Incas (Quechua or Runasimi) are translated or explained in the text. Therefore, the following glossary lists only those words most repeated or those which merit a more detailed explanation.*

Acclla (aqlia)
A young woman chosen to live in the accllahuasi (huasi = house), where she wove fine textiles and remained in chastity.

Apu (apu)
An imposing peak, object of reverence. See God of Water.

Coca (koka)
Shrub the leaves of which were chewed *(Erythroxylon coca)*. It was used in divination, to alleviate tiredness during heavy manual work, and as an offering to supernatural powers. In contrast to the chewed (chacchada) leaf, which is then spat out after its nutrients and trace elements of alkaloid have been absorbed, the drugs derived from coca leaves concentrate the alkaloid via harmful chemical agents, and are addictive. In ancient Peru, and still among present-day rural people, coca leaves were only chewed.

God of Water
The most important Andean deity. Feared and worshipped due to the atmospheric conditions under his control. Illapa, Pachacámac, Apu and even Inti (Sun), seem to have been nothing more than personifications of the God of Water, according to Kauffmann Doig.

Earth Goddess
Known to this day as Pachamama. The counterpart of the God of Water and the direct source of food, as long as the God of Water fertilized her by soaking her with his rains at the correct time.

Huairana (wairana)
A three-walled construction (from huayra = air or wind)

Inca (inka)
Sovereign. Name of the ethnic group based in the Cuzco valley. Also a synonym for the Inca state, usually used to refer to the population as well as the dynasty.

Inca Ñan (inka-nian = road)
See Qhapaq Ñan.

Inca State
(Incario). The state forged by the ethnic group known as the Incas, stretching from Ancasmayo in Colombia to Maule in Chile. All the ethnic groups incorporated shared common traditions and were, to a degree, related.

Intihuatana (Intiwatana)
Translated as "the place where the Sun is tied down" and used to describe a type of altar.

Mitmac
Person or ethnic group transferred by order of the state from one area to inhabit another. The first chroniclers used the term "mitmae".

Qhapaq Ñan
Inca state highway. (Qhapaq = hierarchy, ñan = road). The road network covered more than 23,000 kilometres.

Quechua (qetshwa)
The main language of the Inca state. Originally known as Runasimi, "the language of the people". The term comes from the name of the eponymous ecological region of inter-Andean valleys between 2000 and 3000 metres above sea level.

Quero (qero)
A painted, wooden ceremonial cup manufactured since the 16th century by indigenous artisans. They imitate European drawing and show scenes representing the customs and spirituality of the Andean people. Those made from gold or silver are known as aquillas (aquilias).

Quipu (qipu)
Mnemonic system based on knotted cords.

Tahuantinsuyo
The "four directions", or regions which together formed the Inca state. See Inca state (tawa = four, suio = direction or region).

Ushnu
Throne. Also has other accepted meanings.

---

* With regard to how Quechua words should be written, we have opted for the traditional form (i.e., Inca and not Inka). However, in cases where universally recognised phonetic spellings, particularly in the case of archaeological sites, use k instead of c, or w instead of hu, we have adopted those usages.

Suggested Reading

ANGLES VARGAS (Víctor)
2000   Machu Picchu and the Inca Road / Machu Picchu y el camino inca. Lima.

BINGHAM (Hiram)
1930   Machu Picchu / A Citadel of the Incas. New York.
1948   Lost City of the Incas / the Story of Machu Picchu and its Builders. New York.
2002   Lost City of the Incas / The Story of Machu Picchu and its Builders (With an introduction by Hugh Thomson). London.

BURGER (Richard L.) y Lucy C. SALAZAR, eds.
2004   Machu Picchu - Unveiling the Mystery of the Incas (Yale University Press). New Haven and London.

BUSE DE LA GUERRA (Hermann)
1978   Machu Picchu. Lima.

FROST (Peter) et al. - Jim BARTLE (Ed.)
1995   Machu Picchu Historical Sanctuary / Cusco, Peru. Lima.

GASPARINI (Graziano) y MARGOLIES (Luise)
1980   Inka Architecture (Indiana University Press). Bloomington.

GONZÁLEZ (Elena) y Rafael LEÓN (Editores)
2001   Machu Picchu: Santuario histórico / Historical Sanctuary (Photographs Jorge H. Esquiroz). AFP Integra. Lima.

GUILLÉN GUILLÉN (Edmundo)
1994   La guerra de la reconquista inka. Lima.

KAUFFMANN DOIG (Federico)
1987   "Indians of the Andes". The Encyclopedia of Religion edited by Mircea Eliade et al. 13, pp. 465-472 (Macmillan Publishing Company). New York.

2001   Sex and Sexual Magic in Ancient Peru. Lima.
2002   Historia y arte del Perú antiguo, 6 vs. Lima.
2003   "Andean Gods: Gods of Sustenance". Precolombart 4/5 (2001-2002), pp. 55-69. Barcelona.

HEMMING (John)
1970   The Conquest of the Incas (Harcourt Brace Jovanovich). New York.

LEE (Vincent R.)
2000   Forgotten Vilcabamba / Final Stronghold of the Incas (Sixpac Manco Publications). Wyoming.

REINHARD (Johan)
2002   Machu Picchu / The Sacred Center (Published by Machu Picchu Institute / Editorial coordinator Jim Bartle). Lima.

ROWE (John H.)
1990   "Machupijchu a la luz de documentos del siglo XVI". Histórica 14 (1), pp. 139-154. Lima.

TORD (Luis Enrique)
1975   Guide to Machu Picchu / including one plan one map, 8 color plates and 14 photographs (Introduction Duccio Bonavia). Lima.

VALCÁRCEL (Luis E.)
1964   Machu Picchu el más famoso monumento arqueológico del Perú. Buenos Aires.

VEGA (Juan José)
1980   Incas contra españoles / treinta batallas. Lima.

WRIGHT (Ruth M.) y Alfredo VALENCIA ZEGARRA
2001   The Machu Picchu Guide Book / A Self-Guide Tour. Boulder, Colorado.

WUST (Walter)
2003   Inca Guide to Cuzco / Touring in the Heart of the Land of the Incas. Lima.

Index

Federico Kauffmann Doig. The author was born in Chiclayo, Peru. While on his father's side he is descended from German stock, his mother's ancestors came from the ancient Moche, or Mochica culture. He holds a doctorate in archaeology, as well as a second doctorate in history. Both degrees were awarded by the Universidad Mayor de San Marcos in Lima. He has also been awarded three doctorates Honoris Causa.

Founding director of the Museum of Art, he was also Director of the National Museum of Archaeology in Lima. He divides his time between research into Peru's past and his duties as a lecturer at several of the nation's universities. As a visiting professor at the University of Bonn he taught Peruvian and American archaeology.

His prolific professional work has been honoured with the title Amauta, the highest award given by Peru in the field of culture. He has twice received Peru's Premio Nacional de Cultura, and was the first Latin American to be awarded Sweden's Neubergh Medal. He has been decorated by the Peruvian government, as well as by the governments of Belgium, Austria and Sweden.

He is a member of Peru's National Academy of History, an Honorary Member of the Barbier-Mueller Museum in Switzerland, a Member of the Royal Academy of History in Madrid, and the founding director of the Institute of Amazonian Archaeology.

He belongs to the Scientific Committee of the Centro Studi Ricerche Ligabue, in Venice, and, together with Giancarlo Ligabue, has made 14 expeditions to the Peruvian Amazonian Andes, as well as to other archaeological sites in the regions of Cajamarca, Ancash, Arequipa, Madre de Dios etc.

Kauffmann Doig is the author of several works, including Manual of Peruvian Archaeology, which ran to ten editions; as well as the following books: Sex and Sexual Magic in Ancient Peru (2001), The Chachapoyans (2003). His book, History of Art in Ancient Peru, published in six volumes in Lima (2002), is the most complete and detailed work to date on the subject.

The North Amazon Circuit

Machu Picchu is without a doubt the jewel of ancient Peruvian architecture and the great symbol of all things Peruvian. But Machu Picchu is not all that Peru has to offer, for many other imposing monuments were built in the Andes and on the Pacific coast. Tarapoto and Alto Mayo are just two of the many corners of Peru which offer visitors spectacular natural scenery, while the departments of Amazonas and San Martin are home to the many archaeological sites that are the great vestiges of the Chachapoyas culture. These fascinating places are part of the North Amazon Circuit.

The Chachapoyas Culture
Federico Kauffmann Doig

When the Spanish arrived in Peru the Chachapoyas were one of the many "nations" that formed the Inca state, or Tahuantinsuyo. At the time, the Chachapoyas were made up of several groups, and their differences were more political and territorial than cultural or linguistic. In fact, despite their differences, the similarities apparent in the architectural remains scattered throughout the region stand as testament to the cultural links between these groups, as described by the chroniclers of the 16th century. The territory of the Chachapoyas extended for 400 kilometres from north to south, occupying the present-day departments of Amazonas and San Martin, as well as the eastern edge of La Libertad, and the culture occupied areas between 2000 and 3000 metres above sea level.

The historian Pedro Cieza de León (1553) offers a number of colourful details in his description of the Chachapoyas. He describes them as "the whitest and most handsome of all the peoples I have seen in the Indies through which I have travelled, and their women were so beautiful that many of them were chosen by the Incas and taken to the temples of the sun (…)". He goes on to say that "they and their husbands dressed in woollen clothing and wore *llautos* on their heads, by which they were recognised wherever they went". In terms of the structure of their society, the Chachapoyas were basically divided into two strata: the ruling class and their subjects. Their colossal public works, such as Kuélap, are indisputable testaments to this social model, without which they simply would never have existed. Whether we like it or not, it is a fact that humanity's ancient civilisations developed by virtue of their rigid class structure.

The many territorial groups that formed the Chachapoyas "nation" would have had their own leaders, a fact which does not exclude the existence of fairly powerful "fiefdoms" which flourished in areas such as that occupied by the Chillchos, the Chillao and the inhabitants of the river basins of Abiseo (Pajatén) and Huabayacu-Huayllabamba (Gran Saposoa). Conflicts to maintain predominance and manoeuvring to form alliances were the order of the day, according to 16th century historical sources. In this sense, the Chachapoyas were no different to the other generally bellicose "nations" spread throughout the territory of ancient Peru before their incorporation into the Inca state, and such conflicts would continue to some degree for centuries to come under Spanish dominion, in the form of disputes over land between "caciques" or "curacas" (native local governors). It is likely that internal tensions among the Chachapoyas would diminish or even disappear temporarily in the face of a common threat from an outside enemy, given that they were conscious of the cultural links and common ancestral lands that united them. Such a view is supported by the evidence of the stubborn resistance mounted by the Chachapoyas in the face of the advance of the Inca forces bent on conquering their territory.

In terms of the role played in society by each class, we can state categorically that among the Chachapoyas those who formed the ruling class assumed the primary responsibility of safeguarding food production surplus. An agricultural surplus was considered indispensable in order to confront the years when crops failed - a recurring problem due to the El Niño phenomenon.

The El Niño affected agriculture adversely, for production was based on non-irrigated land dependent on regular seasonal rains. The elite were also in charge of "state rituals". These took place at administration centres such as Kuelap, which had areas reserved for worship and ceremonies. Rituals would have been directed above all at exorcising the recurrent atmospheric calamities affecting production unleashed by the El Niño phenomenon, which not only affected the inhabitants of the Coastal Andes and the Andean Highlands, but also the Chachapoyas of the Amazonian Andes. In fact, in the Amazonian Andes too the seasonal rains are

Opposite page:
◄
Frontispiece of Kuelap viewed from the air

◄
A Chachapoyas face painted on a wall

◄
Chachapoyas woman in traditional clothing

◄
Part of an enormous Chachapoyas textile

Photos Federico Kauffmann Doig

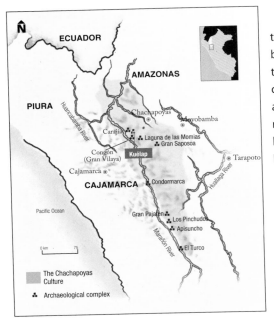

The Chachapoyas Culture

♣ Archaeological complex

often early or late, and landslides are produced by excessive rainfall*.

The author has dedicated careful study to efforts to establish the origin of the Chachapoyas culture. Although there is evidence of human settlement in the region they occupied going back some 8000 years before their emergence, the Chachapoyas culture itself began to develop from around the second half of the first millennium after Christ. Such a hypothesis assumes that the people who occupied what would become the territory of the Chachapoyas moved

(*) These and other conclusions reached by the author with regard to the Chachapoyas culture have been examined in specialist monographs. These publications have been gathered together in the book "Los Chachapoyas / moradores ancestrales de los Andes Amazónicos peruanos", a 485 page volume published in 2003 by the Universidad Alas Peruanas, Lima.

there from the Andes. This theory is based on the fact that elements of the Chachapoyas culture are of Andean rather than Amazonian origin, although of course their new environment, so different from the highlands, meant that new modes of behaviour emerged, such as the pattern represented by the funerary statues that remain to this day, and analysis of which indicates that they were inspired by Tiahuanaco-Huari funerary bundles (Middle Horizon period).

We will describe later some of the Chachapoyas archaeological sites of particular interest scattered all over the present-day departments of Amazonas and San Martín.

KUELAP

Located on the left bank of the Utcubamba River in the department of Amazonas, Kuelap is the name of an archaeological site remarkable for the enormous scale of its architecture. The construction dates from approximately 1000 AD, when the Chachapoyas culture was flourishing.

Through his studies of Kuelap in the context of pre-Hispanic architecture, the author has concluded that the site was not a fortress, but rather a great administration centre for the production of foodstuffs and the performance of the rites the inhabitants believed essential to that production.

This representative example of Chachapoyas architecture remained unknown to the outside world until 1843, when Juan Crisostomo Nieto was guided to the site by locals who had

always known of the existence of the magnificent ruins. Subsequently, Kuelap would draw the attention of a few scholars and other visitors interested in antiquities, the most notable of whom were Adolf Bandelier, Louis Langlois and Henry Reichlen.

The ruins of Kuelap are situated on the summit of a hill at the following geographical coordinates: 6° 24' 26" and 77° 54' 16", according to the engineer Herman Corbera.

Kuelap is monumental in character. The site comprises a great platform, running from south to north and set on a crest of calcareous rock. The platform is almost six hundred metres long and is sustained by an up to nineteen metre-high wall.

Upon this platform and to one side stands a second level platform with four hundred buildings on it, most of which are circular. Of the majority of these buildings, only the bases remain. In some cases, the buildings have walls decorated with friezes with symbolic designs. The majority of these do not seem to have been dwellings, but rather storerooms for foodstuffs for the inhabitants who suffered recurrent food shortages when the region was periodically lashed by natural disasters unleashed by the El Niño phenomenon. The peasant class would have dwelled in the fields around the site, but the fragile structures of their houses have not survived the ravages of time.

Among the many structures at Kuelap there are three that stand out: the Tintero ("inkwell"), the Atalaya ("watchtower") and the Castillo (castle).

The Tintero is situated at the extreme southern end of the great platform. It is a circular tower conceived in the form of an inverted cone - a structure that seems to defy gravity. The engineer Uwe Carlson is of the opinion that this inclination has developed due to subsidence and was not originally intended. The Atalaya is a tower, and is located at the northernmost part of Kuelap. The Castle is located in the most conspicuous part of the complex and was probably home to society's highest ranking dignitaries.

Access to the first platform was only possible via two doorways, both of them located in the western, or main, façade; a third door, located to one side of a west-facing cliff, would have been an "exit" to the cliff, rather than an entrance; its location suggests it led to an area used for offerings and sacrifices.

The best-preserved, and probably the principal doorway, is located on the south side of the west-facing façade. The base of this doorway is three metres wide and its jambs taper to the entrance's full height of ten metres. To facilitate access to the platform already mentioned, this doorway cuts through the platform, leaving a wedge-shaped hole: perhaps this structure was meant to symbolise the vagina of the Earth Goddess.

Upon entering, the visitor is led along a passageway in the form of a ramp flanked by high walls and resembling an alleyway. This space becomes narrower along its twenty-metre length until it is finally just wide enough to allow one person to pass at a time, like a narrow tunnel. Although the jambs almost touch at their highest part, the sidewalls of the passageway produce an "alleyway", roofless, with the walls inclined inwards.

Clearly, Kuelap existed before the rise of the Inca state. Given its monumental character, it doubtless performed an important role in the history of the Chachapoyas culture. In fact, Kuelap's architecture is, in general terms, the same as that found throughout the territory occupied by the Chachapoyas culture. What has not been established to date is in what moment of the long process of the development of the Chachapoyas culture, which may have begun as early as the 8th century, Kuelap was constructed. Nor do we know for how long Kuelap flourished or when and why it was abandoned.

There are other aspects of Kuelap which have not been clarified: the effort needed for the construction of a site as enormous as Kuelap and the skill of the engineers who were able to provide it with a sophisticated drainage system. Today, because the ducts are blocked, the site shows signs of wear. The great platform has swollen and the stones of the walls that surround it are working loose. The great majority of the buildings would have been food stores.

No completely satisfactory explanation of Kuelap's function has yet been proposed. The site is popularly described as a "fortress", due to its location and the height of the walls that support the main platform. Adolf Bandelier, and particularly Louis Langlois, tried to demonstrate that Kuelap, rather than just a fortress, was actually a fortified place designed as a refuge for the local

population in case of emergency. They drew an analogy between the function of Kuelap and that of the fortified towns of medieval Europe.

By taking into account the function of monumental architecture in the Peruvian past in general – which was related to the socio-economic necessities of the time – it can be concluded that Kuelap was basically a pre-Inca sanctuary where the powerful aristoc-

Entrance to the Kuelap platform and one of the four hundred buildings sited on it and recently restored. **Photos Federico Kauffmann Doig**

racy resided, carrying out the primary mission of managing food production and overseeing the magical practices designed to ensure the cooperation of the supernatural powers that governed atmospheric phenomena, and which, when not correctly honoured, could bring excessive rains or drought to bear that threatened human existence.

THE SARCOPHAGI OF KARAJIA

Although the Chachapoyas custom of using sarcophagi (coffins that followed the human form) to bury their dead was first mentioned as early as 1791 (in the Mercurio Peruano), and interested Louis Langlois (1939) and the archaeologists Henry and Paule Reichlen (1950), this funerary practice was subsequently practically forgotten. In 1985, an expedition led by Federico Kauffmann Doig managed to locate, at Karajia, the most important group of sarcophagi discov-

ered to date and preserved intact. We reached the site through information provided by Carlos Torres Mas.

The sarcophagi of Karajia-1 are unique in terms of their colossal size - they are up to 2.50m high – and also their careful design. Thanks to the assistance of members of the Peruvian Andean Club, the archaeologists were able to scale the 24m vertical rock wall and access the cave where the sarcophagi had been placed, some 200m above the bottom of the ravine. Karajia-1 comprises seven sarcophagi. The eighth was demolished at some time – probably during the earthquake of 1928 – and collapsed into the abyss. Because the sarcophagi were joined side by side, the collapse of the eighth structure opened holes in the sides of its neighbours. This event permitted the study of the contents of these tombs and conclusions to be drawn regard-

ing the content of the other sarcophagi without the need to violate them in any way. Inside the opened sarcophagi a mummy was found, seated on an animal hide and wrapped in funerary garments. Pottery objects and several offerings accompanied the deceased. Radiocarbon dating of the organic remains produced the date of 1460 AD + 60. Rodents and scavenging birds had disturbed the tomb. Sarcophagus 1 was empty because the mummy and its offerings had been devoured and dragged from the chamber. The sarcophagi are shaped like large anthropomorphic capsules, and were modelled from clay mixed with twigs and stones. Only the head and part of the chest are solid. Both the head and the body are decorated with two-toned red paint applied over a white base.

We believe that these sarcophagi are evocative of the type of funerary bundle typical to the coast and highlands during the Tiahuanaco-Huari period. In both cases, the anthropomorphic form only follows the shape of the human trunk, without repre-

The Karajia Group 1 during the study of the site. (Photos: Giancarlo Ligabue and Federico Kauffmann Doig).

Comparison of a Chachapoyas sarcophagus with a funerary bundle from the Middle Horizon period. The former would seem to have been inspired by the latter.

Drawings: Bernardino Ojeda and Aníbal Santiváñez

Photos Pajaten: Pedro Rojas Ponce. Drawings and Chancay textile photo: Federico Kauffmann Doig.

One of the circular buildings of Gran Pajaten decorated with females figures. **Photo courtesy Duccio Bonavia.**

Note how one of the figures wears a headdress shaped like a bird's wings, similar to the bird images seen on another building at Pajatén (drawing below).

The human figure in the photo, taken from a textile in the Museo Amano, shows a feathered headdress, and resembles some of the human figures found at Pajatén.

senting the extremities. It should be pointed out that the heads of the sarcophagi are sculptural, and that the faces are the result of clay copies of funeral masks originally made from wood cut in a half-moon shape to represent the jaw.

Other groups of sarcophagi, such as those of Tingorbamba and Chipuric, located nearby, have been well-documented by the expeditions led by the author.

GRAN PAJATEN

The ruins of Gran Pajaten were discovered in 1963 by a group of villagers from Pataz who ventured into the surrounding Amazonian Andean region. Ostensibly, they were in search of land and pasture, but it is believed they actually crossed the high plains and travelled down into the forested eastern slopes of the Andes in search of a "lost city" and its gold, hidden in the thick tropical foliage.

What is certain is that this was no mere legend, for the group did in fact come across architectural remains in an area popularly believed to have been the lo-cation of a lost city. However, the walls were not made of gold or silver as they had hoped. Nevertheless, the find was a sensational one, given the singular nature and majesty of the architectural complex they discovered.

Gran Pajaten is situated on a tributary of the Abiseo river basin, at 2,850 metres above sea level, in the province of Mariscal Caceres (San Martin). It was not located, as had first been thought, on the Pajaten River. The Abiseo River, a tributary of the Huallaga, was once known as the Apisuncho and also the Unamizo.

The ruins of Gran Pajaten comprise some twenty circular chambers which, given their architectural design, must have belonged to the Chachapoyas culture, which emerged near the 8th century and was incorporated into the Inca state around 1470 AD. According to the author's hypothesis, the culture grew from migrations from the highlands to the Amazonian Andes, centuries before the rise of the Inca state, of groups in search of agricultural land, due to the fact that in Peru land suitable for cultivation is limited and increasing population levels meant solutions had to be found.

The constructions at Gran Pajaten are towers typical of Chachapoyas architecture. The walls exhibit decorative elements. These are remarkable in that they ingeniously present the desired motifs with blocks that are part of the walls themselves. The only anatomical motif represented sculpturally is the head.

The most spectacular iconographic motifs are those found at chambers 1 and 5. These are female anthropomorphic figures, which appear seated, with their knees apart as if they were about to give birth. Their abdomens are swollen like those of pregnant women. The author has classified these human figures as anthropomorphic representations of Pachamama, the Earth Goddess. Usually, Pachamama was not represented in human form in ancient Peru, but rather with a stepped symbol alluding to agricultural terracing.

The figures of Pachamama at Gran Pajaten are shown in a row, one next to another. The position of their arms suggests wings, as if they were capable of flight.

The figures are posed nude, but they wear enormous headdresses of two types: while one seems to represent a feathered headdress, the other is shaped like the wings of a bird about to take flight. The author noticed a similarity between these designs and others representing birdlike figures with outspread wings in Chamber 2 of Gran Pajaten.

The ruins of Gran Pajaten have been the subject of archaeological research on four occasions: The first was in 1965, by an expedition led by Victor Pimentel and Pedro Rojas Ponce; the second, in 1966, included the archaeologist Duccio Bonavia and provided a detailed description of the site; the third was led by Federico Kauffmann Doig on trips made in 1980, 1982 and 1986, and concentrated on the series of mausoleums near Gran Pajaten, known as Los Pinchudos; the fourth research project was organised by the University of Boulder, Colorado, and it discovered a new complex in the vicinity, now known as Cerro Central, as well as evidence of human occupation prior to the Chachapoyas, according to Tom Lennon and, more particularly, Warren Church.

THE LOS PINCHUDOS MAUSOLEUMS

When in 1980 we travelled through the area of Gran Pajaten, in the River Abiseo Park, we came across mausoleums on the outside walls of which were hung anthropomorphic woodcarvings. These remains were already known to our guide, Manuelasho, who had visited the site in 1976. They had also been referred to by the archaeologists Jaime Deza Rivasplata and, earlier, Duccio Bonavia, who made reference to rumours which had reached the ears of Victor Pimentel Gurmendi. However, they were not lucky enough to be able to visit this archaeological marvel. After our first reconnaissance, in 1980, we returned three times to Los Pinchudos and made the first studies of the site.

The anthropomorphic woodcarvings were intact and in their original location, except for one, which shortly before our arrival had been cut from its place with a machete.

The Los Pinchudos mausoleums are situated at 2,800 metres above sea level in dense forest. They are protected by a cave cut from the side of a ravine. The microclimate in the cave has meant that the wood has not been adversely affected by the humid environment of the forest. Other factors have also contributed to their good state of preservation, such as the hardwood used by their creators and the fact that they were originally covered with a fine layer of clay and and possibly painted in the manner of Chimu idols.

Seven mausoleums form the Los Pichudos site. Their walls were built from slabs of slate. The internal walls are decorated with motifs formed by projecting stones. The walls were also covered with coloured clay of varying tones. These iconographic elements are similar to those found at Gran Pajaten and permit us to speculate that its walls were also originally painted. The decorative motifs are in the form of friezes, and we were able to distinguish the symbol of water, which is the crest of a wave, a design very common in Andean iconography.

The funerary bundles placed in these mausoleums were looted long ago. The majority of the fragments of pottery found at the site are in the style of Cuzco ceramics, which would seem to indicate

The anthropomorphic carvings are anchored to the upper section of the wall. The stake and the idol are carved from the same piece of wood. The five idols *in situ*, which are each about 60 centimetres tall, are of a very hard and heavy wood. The carvings represent naked men with bulging genitals. Their arms and hands rest on their chests and the legs are slightly flexed. This is a universal image in Andean iconography: an emblematic form linking the human figure to that of a feline, with its paws raised.

Drawings Roberto Samanez; Photo Gustavo Siles

that Inca expansionism reached as far as the area of Gran Pajaten. But the mausoleums of Los Pichudos are of Chachapoyas manufacture, and were probably still being used during the Inca period for the burial of Inca administrators.

THE LAKE OF THE MUMMIES

In the middle of the cloak of thick tropical vegetation that covers the rolling slopes of the Amazonian Andes, where humankind never established itself, workers from the Ullilén ranch in Leimebamba, in the department of Amazonas saw by chance, at the beginning of 1997, a group of pre-Inca mausoleums. Little did they know that these important funerary constructions jealously guarded in their interior a true archaeological miracle.

On learning of the existence of that forgotten necropolis, thanks to the diffusion of the news by the journalist Alvaro Rocha, we immediately began to organise an expedition.

It was in May 1997 that the first expedition including professional archaeologists, after the inspection by staff from the city of Chachapoyas office of the National Institute of Culture, left for that remote site. The expedition was led by the author and supported by the Peruvian government through PROMPERU.

From Leimebamba to the site of the mausoleums is some fifteen hours, the first half of which can be made by mule. From there, the route becomes more difficult, with dangerous swamps and the thick tropical vegetation of uninhabited virgin forest which it is only possible to travel through on foot.

Surrounded by a sepulchral silence, the mausoleums occupy a natural cave difficult to access, in the wall of a cliff that rises from a lake unnamed on geographical maps of the region but now popularly known as the Lake of the Mummies. The tombs themselves resemble dwellings, and were built by the ancient Chachapoyas to inter their deceased nobles.

The mausoleums of the Lake of the Mummies were filled with a total of approximately two hundred funerary bundles. Only a small number had been removed by the workers from Ullilén, who stopped their looting when they found none of the gold they had hoped for. This virtually undisturbed site was therefore an authentic archaeological miracle.

The recommendations made in writing to the National Institute of Culture by the author that only a few of the mummies be removed from the mausoleums for study and the rest be left in their original positions, were ignored. The funerary bundles were all taken from their mausoleums and transferred by mule to Leimebamba, where they are now housed in the local site museum.

The funerary bundle consists of a mummy in a seated position, wrapped in textiles both plain and decorated. The process of mummification would have involved sophisticated techniques, judging by the excellent results obtained in such a humid climate.

The mausoleums housed the remains of members of the Chachapoyas culture's highest-ranking members and, in some cases, of their prematurely deceased

The Lake of the Mummies: The upper floor of each mausoleum had a window with jambs, lintel and threshold formed from monolithic blocks. The windows are slightly trapezoidal in shape and were designed to allow a flow of air that prevented the funerary bundles from disintegrating in the humid atmosphere. **Photos Federico Kauffmann Doig**

offspring. During the Inca's dominion of the region, Cuzco-born functionaries who had lived in Cochabamba, a day's journey from the Lake of the Mummies, were also interred at the site in keeping with Chachapoyas traditions. The funerary chambers of the mausoleums have three walls, with the fourth side formed by the cliff face. They are some six metres high and are two-storey. In each chamber were piled, on a kind of dais, some thirty funerary bundles.

Six mausoleums form Group 1 of the Lake of the Mummies. Built with joined masonry, the exterior walls were covered with a white clay paste which was then painted in some parts with red bands.

Gran Saposoa, another Chachapoyas group located at 2,800 metres above sea level on the banks of the Huabayacu River, in the basin of the rivers Yonan, Huayllabamba, Huabayacu and Bravo – an area visited by Gene Savoy and the Peruvian archaeologists Alberto Bueno and Miguel Cornejo and explored many years earlier by Keith Muscutt, Inge Schjelerup and Peter Lerche. **Photo courtesy Anselmo Lozano**

The region boasts an incredible diversity of flora and fauna, especially avifauna. Centre: a rare Yellow-tailed Woolly Monkey *(Lagothrix flauvicauda)*
**Drawings of birds courtesy
Puerto Palmeras Tarapoto Resort.
Photo: Mariella Leo**

Nature
The Magical Corners of Tarapoto and Alto Mayo

The North Amazon Circuit penetrates the eternal green of the Amazon basin, with its exuberant flora and fauna. From Chiclayo, it crosses the imposing Andes mountains and descends through a region of remarkable biodiversity

The areas of Tarapoto and Alto Mayo are rich in species of exotic orchids and hundreds of species of birds – including a stunning variety of hummingbirds, and deep in the Amazon forest are lagoons and lakes where the calls of endemic avifauna provide a singularly exotic symphony.

LAGO LINDO:
JEWEL OF AMAZONIAN NATURE

"Searching for a pristine area", says Claire Jaureguy(*)", an hour and a half from the city of Tarapoto we arrived at the village of Sauce. We crossed the calm lake to its southern shore. This zone is the private property of Carlos González, who in order to conserve the area has created an eco-tourism reserve. He is also the owner of the traditional Hotel Puerto Palmeras and Puerto Patos in Tarapoto."

The Lake Lindo reserve covers an area of 1,700 hectares, and its lodge delights visitors with its location in the midst of this natural paradise. "We reached our destination", continues Jaureguy, "an Amazonian Eden appeared before us. Lago Lindo retains the wild essence of the for-est, the vegetation surrounds it like an ode to water (…) Lago Lindo is an ideal place for bird watching from boats close to its seemingly inaccessible shores".

In her description of Lake Lindo, Jaureguy goes on to explain that both amateur and specialist bird watchers are able to enjoy the local avifauna – listening to them and seeing them in their rich variety of shapes, sizes and colours as they fly over the forest, build their nests and mate. Among the species that inhabit the forest around the lake are: the Golden-collared Toucanet (Selenidera reinwardtii); the Green Kingfisher (Chloroceryle americana); the Shansho or Hoatzin (Opisthocomus hoazin), with its cat-like call; Many-banded Aracari (Pteroglossus pluricinctus), with its bright yellow and black plumage: the large and elegant Anhinga (Anhinga anhinga) and the Swallow-tailed Kite (Elanoides forficatus), which flies like a tiny comet. To see all of these species and many more, one need only take a dip in the warm waters of the lake with its limpid reflections of the surrounding forest, or row a small boat silently across its surface.

The area of the reserve, adds Jaureguy, has trails "for walks anyone can do. Deep in the forest we forgot our insatiable thirst and the mosquitoes because we were learning about the workings of the tropical forest, the im-portance of the existence of each tree in the lives of hundreds of species, from the smallest fungi and termites to the Red-crested Woodpecker (Campephilus melanoleucos). We soon reached the lake viewpoint, from where we were able to see Lago Lindo or Suni Cocha and Limon Cocha, the saltwater lake".

"The design of the lodge at Lake Lindo maintains a harmony with the lush and charming scenery. Wooden bungalows each house four people and are ideal for relaxation after a day on the lake, lying in a swinging hammock and processing the information learned about the forest while its inhabitants go on with their lives all around you".

(*) El Comercio 7-XI-2005

Lago Lindo. **Photo Antonio Escalante**
www.puertopalmeras.com

THE FAMOUS COCK-OF-THE-ROCK

The cock-of-the-rock (Rupicola peruviana) is one of the most spectacular and well-known birds of Peru. It inhabits the lower montane forest below 2,000m. This large orange fruit-eater can often be seen feeding in fruit trees but is most impressive when seen at a lek. Here males gather at traditional sites in the early morning to display by calling loudly and dancing, bending their heads forward and raising their wings.
The duller females visit the leks to select a mate, who after mating plays no further part in nesting or feeding the young.
Photo courtesy Heinz Plenge

A PARADISE OF BIRDS AND ORCHIDS
(Bob Williams/extract*)

The Alto Mayo is an incredibly diverse area that contains a large number of different habitats and consequently an incredible diversity of birds. The whole area and complete range of habitats are traversed by a major road allowing access to all the habitats and to the entire range of bird species of the region, making it one of the best birding destinations in Peru and the world.

A series of small ridges are the home to two of the least known and most sought after bird species in the Alto Mayo; the Long-whiskered Owlet and the Ochre-fronted Antpitta. These two birds have gained almost legendary status. The owl is the world's smallest owl and has only ever been seen when captured in mist nets.

(*) Courtesy: Agencia de Cooperación Técnica Alemana (GTZ)

The Humming-bird Rufous-breasted Hermit (Glaucis hirsuta) The hummingbirds known as Hermits are dull plumaged with long curved beaks specially adapted to feed on specific plants, such as the flowers of the genus *Heliconia.* **Photo courtesy Heinz Plenge**

Opposite page: The Humming-bird Booted Racket-tail (Ocreatus underwoodi) A splendid male specimen of the Booted Racket-tail is feeding on nectar. This hummingbird is noteworthy for both its beauty and aggressive nature. **Photo courtesy Heinz Plenge**

This area is also the best place to find the very rare Royal Sun Angel hummingbird, as well as a wealth of other montane species. The rivers here are also good for Torrent Ducks and Fasciated Tiger-Herons. Near the town of El Afluente the forests become subtropical in nature and a different collection of bird species are found, including the Cock-of-the-Rock. This large orange fruit-eating bird can best be seen at its traditional lek sites (communal displaying areas).

HUMMINGBIRDS
(Bob Williams/extract*)

Hummingbirds are the jewels of the bird world - small, brightly-coloured gems with wings. Hummingbirds are confined to the Americas and in total there are some 328 species, making them one of the largest bird families. Peru supports a staggering 127 species (39% of all hummingbirds), of which some 44 occur in the Alto Mayo region. Hummingbirds occur in all the habitats of the region, from high montane forests to the flooded forests of Tingana, and can even be found in towns and agricultural areas.

The montane forests of the Alto Mayo hold the biggest concentration of species and are also home to some of the more spectacular species such as the Booted Racket-tail and the Long-tailed Sylph, as well as the very rare and local Royal Sun Angel. The lower forests around Moyobamba and flooded forests nearby have slightly fewer species but often support high densities of hermits, duller hummingbirds with long curved beaks that primarily feed on the impressive Heliconia flowers.

At 330 metres above sea level, almost in the Amazon lowlands, the 700 kilometre-long paved road from Chiclayo ends in Tarapoto, where the Mayo river joins the Huallaga. Tarapoto can also be reached by air. The area offers two particularly interesting sites for birdwatchers: the deciduous dry forest of the Huallaga river basin and the lowland forest between Tarapoto and Yurimaguas.

ORCHIDS

(José Altamirano /extract*)

Beautiful and enchanting flowers, orchids flourish in the depths of the forest, amid mosses, lichen, ferns, araceae and bromeliads. They are noted for their multiple shapes, colours and fragrances - among the finest to be found in nature. These peculiarities serve as mechanisms for their intimate relationship with their pollinators: insects (bees, flies, and diurnal and nocturnal butterflies) and birds such as hummingbirds. There also exist fungi which generate a symbiotic relationship with some orchids essential for their reproduction.

The more than 3,000 species that exist in Peru (10% of the world total) are an example of nature's creative exuberance. The greatest diversity is found in the cooler rainforests along the eastern slopes of the Andes. The Alto Mayo is considered a centre of great diversity and endemism and although studies have been limited, an estimated 2,000 species are assumed to exist in the area.

In Moyobamba and the surrounding area there exist specialised nurseries, where dedicated floriculturists grow hundreds of orchid species - a veritable feast of shapes, colours, dimensions, textures and fragrances to delight visitors.

The famous *Cattleya rex*, is one of the species endemic to the region. It flowers between the months of September and December and prefers the cloud forests, where it is found as an epiphyte like the majority of orchids at 3 to 15 m above ground.
Photo courtesy Heinz Plenge

Orchid (*Anguloa uniflora*)
Photo courtesy Heinz Plenge

The Emerald Tree Boa (*Corallus caninus*) This harmless arboreal snake is often mistaken for the deadly Two-striped Forest-Pitviper (*Bothriopsis bilineata*), likewise of a green colour and arboreal.
Photo courtesy Heinz Plenge